With
Listening
Hearts

With Listening Hearts

Understanding the Voices of Lesbian and Gay Catholics

By
Peter J. Liuzzi, O.Carm.

Foreword by
Most Reverend Stephen E. Blaire
Bishop of Stockton, California

Paulist Press
New York/Mahwah, N.J.

Library of Congress Cataloging-in-Publication Data

Liuzzi, Peter J.
    With listening hearts : understanding the voices of lesbian and gay Catholics / by
Peter J. Liuzzi ; foreword by Stephen E. Blaire.
        p. cm.
    Includes bibliographical references (p.   ).
    ISBN 0-8091-3983-9 (alk. paper)
    1. Homosexuality—Religious aspects—Catholic Church. I. Title.

BX1795.H66 L58 2000
282'.086'64—dc21

                                                                        00-048326

Published by Paulist Press
997 Macarthur Boulevard
Mahwah, New Jersey 07430

www.paulistpress.com

Printed and bound in the
United States of America

Table of Contents

Dedication

To Father Dominic Savino, O.Carm.,
my dearest friend and fellow friar

Acknowledgments

I want to thank Cardinal Roger Mahony, Archbishop of Los Angeles, for inviting me to be his third director of the Ministry with Lesbian and Gay Catholics, a ministry whose influence and effectiveness extends far beyond the confines of our great archdiocese. I praise the Cardinal for his insistence that lesbian and gay Catholics never be separated from the ordinary life of Catholic people everywhere.

I want to acknowledge lesbian and gay Catholics who simply and boldly lay claim to all that is theirs by reason of their baptism. Only these men and women know how costly their commitment to the church is.

My heartfelt thanks goes to Father Kenneth McGuire, C.S.P., who called my attention to my spoken and written words as worthy of what I hope is a useful and timely book. Father McGuire was tireless in correcting, nuancing and directing the message of this book. When I was overwhelmed by my work at home and on the road, he kept me focused on the completion of the book.

The delicacy and controversy over homosexuality demands a proper understanding of the scope and nuance of church teaching on this subject. I wish to express my gratitude to Father Gerald Coleman, S.S., rector of St. Patrick's Seminary in Menlo Park, California, and to Monsignor Jeremiah McCarthy, rector of St. John's Seminary in Camarillo, California. Both of these men serve on my advisory board. Hopefully, their theological expertise will be reflected in the doctrinal portions of my book.

I acknowledge my administrative assistant and dear friend, Marge Mayer. Through her support and collaboration so many dreams and hopes have been realized. Marge is the mother of five children, one of whom is gay. Her journey with her son Tim has shaped her into a strong example of a listening heart.

I would also add a word of thanks to Flavio Zappitelli, a dear friend from Italy, for his artful and creative illustrations found scattered throughout the pages of my book. Those pictures, together with well chosen selections from the scriptures, invite the reader to bring a spirit of prayer and calm to the mystery of homosexuality.

Finally, I am grateful to my provincial, Father Leo McCarthy, O.Carm., and all the friars of the Most Pure Heart of Mary Province for their support. When I think of my fraternal family, I recall that chant sung on our profession day: *Ecce quam bonum et quam iucundum habitare fratres in unum.* "How good and joyful it is for brothers to dwell together as one." The very name of my book comes from the theme of one of our provincial chapters. The popular image of Carmel is contemplative prayer. Less known but close to the heart of Carmel is the inspiration and imitation of the prophetic life of Elijah found in the Book of Kings. It is that prophetic spirit that shapes my ministry and inspired this book.

Drawings

by Flavio

Foreword

by
Most Reverend Stephen E. Blaire
Bishop of Stockton, California

It is virtually impossible to speak or write about homosexuality without stirring up preconceptions or emotional reactions in the hearer or reader. The Catholic Church's teaching on this subject is clear, but it is received in different ways according to the predispositions of the recipient. Father Peter Liuzzi in his book hopes to acquaint the reader with the faith experience of homosexual persons seeking to find a home in the Catholic Church and to assist their families and friends in understanding this quest. He sets the stage by offering his perspective on the issue of homosexuality, but the import of his book is the homosexual person in relation to the Church. He brings to this discussion his years of study and experience as the director of the Ministry with Gay and Lesbian Catholics in the Archdiocese of Los Angeles. It was while I served as auxiliary bishop of the archdiocese that I came to know and admire Father Liuzzi's work. His book is the personal reflection of a pastoral point of view. Its presuppositions in regard to the nature of homosexuality cannot be pressed to be more than a general survey of the rather turbulent field of current investigation into the origins and realities of homosexuality.

An analogy of the Church's pastoral care for the divorced and remarried might help to understand Father Liuzzi's objective in this book. The Catholic Church, based on the teaching of Jesus, does not accept divorce and remarriage. However, the Church carefully approaches in its pastoral care all the circumstances that might affect a marriage in seeking to help people be reconciled to the Church. The work of the diocesan marriage tribunals well illustrates the Church's pastoral care. However, some people are divorced and remarried outside the Catholic Church with no immediate hope of resolving their marital situation within the Church. Such couples can live as brother and sister and receive the sacraments. But even if they live as husband and wife "civilly married outside the Church" and cannot receive the sacraments, they are welcome to attend Mass and be part of a parish. A rigorist could publicly brand them as adulterers, but the Church in her pastoral care finds a place for them in their "irregular situation."

All analogies limp, but the point of genuine comparison can say that while the Church in no way mitigates its teaching, she nevertheless seeks to care pastorally for all her members, even those in "irregular situations." The Church's moral teaching on homosexual activity is clear and must be upheld in pastoral practice. Each individual's spiritual growth and development must be understood within the context of the whole gospel message of conversion. Pastoral care requires that objective morality always take into account intentionality and circumstances when it comes to subjective moral imputability.

The gay political agenda and the pastoral care of the homosexual person can interconnect positively on some points but often do not. It is inaccurate to accuse the Church and her pastoral ministers of unjust discrimination against gay and lesbian people when she speaks in defense of human rights and dignity for all peoples but cannot support particular agenda items that would violate traditional biblical and Catholic moral principles. It is Catholic teaching that men and women with homosexual orientations be accepted with respect, compassion and sensitivity. The *Catechism of the Catholic Church* states that "every sign of unjust discrimination in their regard should be avoided."

Father Liuzzi's book appreciates the tension homosexual Catholics may find themselves experiencing within the Church, but offers them a place of welcome with all the other baptized. The gospel message is universal and all-encompassing in its call, regardless of whether one is young or old; rich or poor; brown, black, white, red or yellow; male or female; heterosexual or homosexual.

Chapter 1

Everyone Is Talking about It

Why write about homosexuality? The most obvious reason is that most everyone is talking about homosexuality. What is little known is that the bishops of the Roman Catholic Church have been part of the conversation since the 1970s. Many bishops and conferences of bishops have clarified what the church believes and teaches about homosexuality. The same bishops have offered guiding principles to be used in the church's pastoral outreach and inclusion of homosexual Catholics in the life of the church. Unfortunately, many Catholics and even some pastors remain ignorant of such teachings and concerns. In a document from the Congregation for the Doctrine of the Faith, we read:

"For where your treasure is, there also will your heart be." Luke 12:34

> ...it can be clearly seen that the phenomenon of homosexuality, complex as it is, and with its many consequences for society and ecclesial life, is a proper focus for the Church's pastoral care. It thus requires of her ministers attentive study, active concern and honest, theologically well-balanced counsel.[1]

It is my hope that this modest little book will assist Catholic readers everywhere in a better understanding of the controversial and complex reality that is homosexuality. While much writing is done on this subject, much of the literature is often as complex as the subject itself. This present volume is neither an academic nor a theoretical work. It is the result of my efforts to offer a simple and clear presentation of church teaching and the pastoral concerns around homosexuality. This book is not intended as an exhaustive treatment of the subject. Rather, I choose to highlight what I consider some basic information about homosexuality. This book is very much a book for beginners. I would also add, from the very start, that this book adheres strictly to the teachings and sound pastoral practices of the Roman Catholic Church. Perhaps some readers with more knowledge will be disappointed with such fidelity. And still others with clearly more liberal views might be put off altogether. It seems to me that only a clear presentation of what the church teaches and does not teach makes for a more informed and accurate conversation and understanding. Moreover, it seems unfair to give homosexual Catholics anything less than authentic teaching so as to avoid disappointment and anger when they find out otherwise. My fidelity to doctrine is not to deny that there are very important and valid questions about homosexuality that need answers and further discernment. But such questions can easily detract from my main focus, which is primarily a pastoral concern that leads to understanding and solidarity with the plight of homosexual Catholics and their families. I have chosen this approach instead of an emphasis on theoretical questions, which can all too easily degenerate into argumentation and defensiveness.

While the topic is of interest to many Catholics, my hope is to reach mothers and fathers who have homosexual children. I do not pretend to be an expert in the field of homosexuality, even though I have many years of experience ministering with homosexual men and women and their families. In all those years I have learned much that I can share with my readers. Yet, the greatest lesson I have learned is that there is so much more to learn. Some of what we have to learn is about doctrine and morality; some is about what the sciences have to tell us through research results. Most of what we have to learn comes from entering into the lived experience of our homosexual relatives, friends and neighbors. I would only hope that whatever I have learned and can share will lead the reader toward a desire to learn more about something that deeply shapes the lives of so many good people.

For the last ten years I have been the director of the Los Angeles archdiocesan Ministry with Lesbian and Gay Catholics (MLGC). That ministry was established by Cardinal Roger Mahony in 1986. During these years of ministry, I have met hundreds of homosexual Catholic men and women as I have gone from diocese to diocese, giving workshops and conferences and listening to people's questions and concerns. I have discovered people of simple and deep faith. I have recognized great courage and virtue, and I have seen frailty and limitation. I have seen sin and grace, hope and despair. I have heard stories that call for reflection and prayer. I have come to know some wonderful parents at their best and at their worst moments, as they weather the storms and conflicts that accompany the news that one's offspring is homosexual. I have seen too many parents carry their burdens alone and in secret. I have seen tragedy and triumph. I have seen solidarity that witnesses to the reality that we are truly the Body of Christ. I have seen isolation and rejection, even of one's own flesh and blood. Despite it all, I have always found amazing grace and the loving presence of God.

It would be patronizing to say that the homosexual people whom I have come to know are special or better than their heterosexual counterparts. Rather, I would say that the homosexual people I have encountered are ordinary people who lead very ordinary and quiet lives. They are as good and as bad as the rest of humanity, no better and no worse. And it is amazing to see that, despite much adversity, they manage to live healthy and wholesome lives. Homosexual people and heterosexual people share more that unites them than divides them. We can find our way to them through the gifts of presence, listening and honest conversation.

My deepest sorrow and regret is to have discovered how many homosexual Catholics have quietly drifted away from the church. It is interesting to know some of those who have so distanced themselves. Many do not trace their alienation or hurt to a particular event or person. No, many speak of being alienated gradually by silence. No one speaks about homosexuality. The silence is especially felt when, as young persons, they begin to feel in themselves differences that are frightening and impossible to explain. Never is a prayer uttered for them or their concerns in the prayers of intercession during the Mass. Such an omission is especially noticeable because we usually pray for almost everything possible under the sun. Their parents were never prepared to expect or welcome a homosexual child. Some have had a Catholic education from kindergarten through college without hearing one positive word about homosexuality. Silence has many meanings. Silence can be a form of denial of another's presence or existence in the community. This little book is an attempt to break the silence. Its very title, *With Listening Hearts,* suggests a posture of listening and tending to what is not easily put into human language in the first place. The notion of listening with one's heart suggests that what we are to listen to is the *word* that a person is, rather than the *words* she or he speaks.

My book comes to you in the wake and excitement of a most welcome and recent pastoral letter from the Committee on Marriage and Family Life of the National Conference of Catholic

Bishops. The document is called *Always Our Children: A Pastoral Message to Parents of Homosexual Children and Suggestions for Pastoral Ministers.* In general, many Catholics and non-Catholics alike have favorably received this document. The secular media seemed surprised that the Catholic Church could say something positive about homosexual people. Even some gay-rights organizations praised the document as a good first step in bettering communication with and inclusion of homosexual Catholics. In general, the gay movement was supportive but expressed disappointment that no new ground was laid, such as a recognition of "gay marriage." The most negative criticism of the document comes from very conservative Catholics, some of whom have asked for revisions and clarifications that reflect their own agenda regarding homosexuality.

It is very helpful to recognize that every official church document does not carry equal weight or authority. Given this fact, not a few who are unhappy with *Always Our Children* are quick to point out that the document was "only" the work of a committee of the National Conference of Catholic Bishops. These same critics warn those who minister with homosexual Catholics not to give this pastoral letter an authority that it simply does not have. It is certainly true that *Always Our Children* does not carry the same authority as a document from the Congregation for the Doctrine of the Faith. Yet it is an official document that has the clear support of most bishops in the United States. I do not find such argumentation helpful. I would argue that the document's significance lies beyond the question of its ecclesial authority. This document derives its power from the very persons it addresses. For the first time, to my knowledge, parents of homosexual persons are addressed. The letter is written in a language that is easily understood by ordinary people. A pastoral language is used rather than the customary theological jargon so removed from everyday communication. In addressing parents, their role as primary educators of their children is respected, which is not insignificant, because many parents of homosexual persons often feel they have misused their parental responsibilities and caused their children to be homosexual. In this pastoral letter parents are asked to provide a loving and supportive family environment for their homosexual children. They, together with pastoral leaders, are to make the church a safe and nurturing community of faith.

The bishops have related homosexuality and homosexual persons to family life and the rearing of children. I have found that when homosexuality is divorced from the nuclear family and marriage, a pathway is open to violence and fear of homosexual persons, and the marriages and family life of parents are weakened.

For the first time, at the very end of the letter, homosexual Catholics are also addressed in warm and welcoming words that ask them not to abandon their families or their church:

> Though at times you may feel discouraged, hurt or angry, do not walk away from your families, from the Christian Community, from those who love you. In you God's love is revealed. You are always our children.[2]

One could say that a conversation has begun that lies within the parameters of the teachings of the church. It is *Always Our Children* that is one of the inspirations of this book. I hope that my reflections will promulgate the clear and positive message of our bishops and will inspire my readers to actively collaborate with the bishops in creating a better understanding and appreciation of the challenge homosexuality presents to people of faith.

Whose Agenda?

It is difficult to read anything or engage in a conversation about homosexuality that is not shaped and motivated by strong convictions. Nearly everyone I meet seems to come to the subject of homosexuality with some agenda. I speak about agendas by way of caution. Having an agenda is not necessarily a bad thing, as long as it is recognized, named and owned. Our agenda, if hidden from ourselves or disguised before others, can become a wall that separates us from caring and relating with homosexually oriented persons. Agendas can take on an importance and value that closes us off from empathy, compassion and understanding.

I would like to name what I consider to be some common agendas. Some gay activists will not rest until "gay marriages" are recognized and all rights and privileges accorded to heterosexual marriage are granted to gay unions. Some Catholics' energy is directed toward extending the meaning of sexuality to include monogamous and faithful gay unions and toward having such unions be considered as life-giving and as holy as a sacramental marriage. Some Catholics believe that the only proper ministry to homosexual Catholics is one aimed at changing them to a heterosexual orientation through prayer or some other kind of cure or therapy. Others are quite convinced that homosexuality is a perversion that has entered into the very fabric of our Catholic Church. To some, any recognition or gathering of homosexual persons simply encourages this contagion. Still others might tolerate homosexuality, but only as a spiritual and psychological ill that is best left for the confessional or the psychiatrist's office.

Issues versus Agendas

My hope is that we move beyond our agendas and focus on the issues. One key issue is this: How can we remain faithful to the constant and clear teaching of the church around sexuality and still include and be sensitive to the needs of homosexual Catholics? How can we best support our homosexual Catholics in the call to live a chaste life, which is binding on every Catholic according to one's state in life? Hopefully we recognize that the call to discipleship, even for the homosexual Catholic, entails more than chastity and includes what Jesus called "the higher matters of the law." All Christians are called to live just lives. Christians are called to live lives of prayer and worship. Christians are called to lives of simplicity, avoiding materialism and opulence. Christians are called to live lives that are countercultural. Another issue is the church's response to the gay movement and many of the political and ethical questions that such a movement raises in the public and civil debates about homosexuality. The church cannot simply sell out to a movement or to an agenda that completely violates its teachings and beliefs. On the other hand, it seems to me that the church also needs to avoid sweeping condemnations of what some call the "gay agenda." There are certainly areas of concern that are raised in this debate that the church can and should support. *Letter to Bishops* by the Congregation for the Doctrine of the Faith addressed this very question:

> There is an effort in some countries to manipulate the church by gaining the often well-intentioned support of her pastors with a view to changing civil statutes and laws. This is done in order to conform to these pressure groups' concept that homosexuality is at least completely harmless, if not an entirely good, thing.[3]

A Positive Attitude

What is my attitude toward homosexual Catholics? How shall I approach them? How shall I receive them when they come to me? How may I be truly hospitable? I am not sure I know with certitude the answer to these important and basic questions. But I have learned an approach that I find both simple and helpful. Years ago, as a young priest ordained in 1965, all that I ever learned about homosexuality could be found in two pages of notes. These notes were written in Latin, lest anyone outside the seminary read them and be scandalized that such an unmentionable sin was addressed in the seminary. What I learned in those two pages of notes is what many Catholics continue to believe. I learned that homosexuality was to be viewed only in terms of sexual genital activity. Otherwise, it did not exist. Needless to say, any such activity was considered to be against nature and therefore a grave sin. Given such a narrow understanding, pastoral practice on the part of a priest involved doing everything possible to help the homosexual person to avoid this sin at all costs. The ordinary way of avoiding such a sin was the reception of the sacraments, with special attention given to frequent confession. And in those days, it was a common practice for priests to refuse absolution to anyone who could not promise to avoid this sin in the future. Certainly, there were persons of deep faith and courage who fared well under such a pastoral approach. But such an approach often resulted in a permanent alienation from the church. Many homosexual Catholics, having been refused absolution, left the confessional and simply drifted away from the church, never to return.

As I began to deal with homosexual Catholics, my sense was that this approach was much too simplistic for what is a very complex reality. I began to think that such an approach might not be in the best interest of the spiritual life of those who came to me. I thought it might be a wise thing to listen to my homosexual penitents. I would learn to listen with my heart. I invited homosexual people not only to tell their sins, but to talk about their pain, their journeys in faith, the hard questions they had to face and so much more. I would ask them to discern the calls of the Holy Spirit in this or that situation. It was in such a context that I found my way to explaining facets of church teaching that they had never heard of or known.

I began to learn that inviting and listening to homosexual persons tell their stories is both healing and reconciling for the heterosexual and the homosexual as well. God's grace is always being offered in every human story.

It is a common experience of homosexual Catholics that, in the church, they are always spoken *to* or *about;* no one speaks *with* them. I offered a change of approach. We need to listen as well as speak. Listening is the first step. If listening is to be healing at all, it will be accompanied by a sense of awe and respect toward what one hears and receives. Such listening comprises not only a change of attitude toward the homosexual Catholic; it is also a first mark of hospitality and a move away from what is often experienced as hostility. Listening is not about agreeing with all that one hears. Agreeing can be dishonest, condescending and patronizing, or even counterproductive. To disregard the teaching of the church is dishonest and unfair. Avoiding painful realities can really be misleading. On the other hand, a rigid and coldly objective application of the church's teaching can be most discouraging. Doctrine is abused when we turn it into a threat or make it an unreasonable burden. We need to do all we can do to make the church's teaching truly appealing, grace-filled and liberating. We can set the way to prepare good soil for the word of God and church teaching by listening and walking in solidarity with the pain and joy of others. Jesus himself was a listener who ate and drank with sinners. If we claim to have fellowship with him, then we must admit that we ourselves are sinners before we can be his table companions.

A Final Word

This book is really not about homosexuality at all: it is about persons whose sexual orientation is different, not because they choose it to be such but because they discover and acknowledge it as their reality. Though such persons have been too long ignored and made invisible, we need to recall that they are baptized, full members of the Body of Christ, disciples of the Lord and members of the people of God. These latter realities are far more important than being called or considered a homosexual. The *Letter to Bishops* speaks well when it states:

> The human person, made in the image and likeness of God, can hardly be adequately described by a reductionist reference to his or her sexual orientation. Everyone living on the face of the earth has personal problems...talents and gifts as well. Today the church provides a badly needed context for the care of the human person when she refuses to consider the person as a "heterosexual" or a "homosexual" and insists that every person has a fundamental identity: the creature of God and, by grace, his child and heir to eternal life.[4]

Chapter 2

Toward a Definition of Homosexuality

In 1986 Cardinal Roger Mahony established what is now called the Ministry with Lesbian and Gay Catholics. The event was widely publicized and met with joy by those who filled Blessed Sacrament Church on an eventful and memorable day in February. The occasion was the ending of Forty Hours' devotion, with a Mass offered for the intention of those living with HIV/AIDS. The year was 1986. When that event became newsworthy, some asked: A church-run ministry that is supportive and welcoming of lesbian and gay Catholics? How can that be?

When the cardinal founded the Ministry with Lesbian and Gay Catholics, he did two things of significance. First, he established a central office staffed by a full-time priest-director within the archdiocesan offices, thereby sending a clear message that ministry with homosexual persons was part of the pastoral concern of the local church of Los Angeles. Then he issued a clear mission statement which declared that the purpose of the Ministry with Lesbian and Gay Catholics is "to foster a spirit of community and fellowship among gay Catholics so that they can offer and receive mutual support in living out their lives of faith within the church" (Cardinal Mahony, February 2, 1986). The cardinal's decision came out of a pastoral concern that still remains too uncommon. His actions were in line with the magisterial teachings of the Catholic Church. For example, *Persona*

Humana states: "…the human person is so profoundly affected by sexuality that it must be considered one of the factors which give to each individual's life the principle traits that distinguish it" (no. 1). This same declaration further states:

> …it is from sexuality that the human person receives the characteristics which on the biological, psychological and spiritual levels make the person a man or a woman, and thereby largely condition his or her progress towards maturity and insertion into society.[1]

Here the church is reminding us that the gift of sexuality is a powerful force in our lives. Every human person is a sexual person. Sexuality is an integral part of human living and relating. Now imagine what a challenge sexuality is if one is homosexual rather than heterosexual. Obviously, such a condition requires special understanding and pastoral care on the part of the church.

In 1935, in a "Letter to an American Mother" whose son was homosexual, Sigmund Freud wrote:

> Homosexuality is assuredly no advantage, but it is nothing to be ashamed of, no vice, no deprivation, it cannot be classified as an illness. Many highly respected individuals of ancient and modern times have been homosexuals, several of the greatest men among them (Plato, Michelangelo, Leonardo de Vinci, etc.). It is a great injustice to persecute homosexuality as a crime, and cruelty too.[2]

Can we work toward an agreed-upon definition that squares with Catholic teaching? Is homosexuality a chronic condition that leads a man or a woman into compulsive sexual acting out? Is homosexuality a "preference," that is, a choice of action? Are homosexual persons disinterested or hostile toward members of their opposite sex? Are homosexual persons made homosexual by the company they keep? Are homosexual persons made so because they have been sexually abused? Is homosexuality attributed to a general relaxing of moral principles? Is homosexuality a mental disorder, like pedophilia? Can homosexuality be traced to a highly dysfunctional family system? You can find any number of persons who would answer in the affirmative to any of the above questions. And it is this diversity of opinion that makes homosexuality such a difficult topic. I would suggest that these very questions reveal more bias, stereotyping or ignorance than truth.

The definition of homosexuality from the *Encyclopedia of Bioethics* is both clear and accurate and most useful:

> A homosexual person sustains a predominant, persistent and exclusive psychosexual attraction toward members of the same sex. A homosexual person is one who feels sexual desire and a sexual responsiveness to persons of the same sex and who seeks or would like to seek actual sexual fulfillment of this desire by sexual acts with a person of the same sex.[3]

This definition is helpful because it states that homosexuality is an integral part of one's psychosexual makeup. It further adds that homosexual orientation certainly is marked by a predominant and sustained interest in the same sex but does not exclude all interest in the opposite sex. The definition, like many official Catholic documents, makes a distinction between attraction and desire for sexual activity as opposed to acting on such attractions and desires. This last thought is very important, because one can be homosexual and still be without any genital experience; this is also true of any heterosexual man or woman. A chaste widow remains heterosexual. A celibate priest or nun, a chaste engaged person, a chaste teen and a chaste unmarried senior citizen who are heterosexual in orientation remain heterosexual even though they are not engaging in any kind of genital behavior. By the same token, a chaste homosexual person remains homosexual even though he or she is not engaging in homosexual genital activity. I cannot overstate the distinction between feelings of attraction to same-sex activity and acting on those attractions. Sexual orientation and feelings are simply not synonymous with genital activity. And it can also be noted that the church itself makes the distinction between homosexual orientation, which is not a sin, and sexual activity, which is always sinful.

It is equally important and helpful to spell out some other significant nuances and distinctions. A homosexual person is one who sustains all of the characteristics mentioned in the definition of the *Encyclopedia of Bioethics*, but every homosexual man or woman does not express his or her orientation in the same way. Some homosexual persons are quite content to use the word *homosexual* to define their orientation or inclination, but many such people are also content and even prefer not to acknowledge that reality in their public lives for any number of reasons that may be healthy or unhealthy. Very often, but not always, the use of the term *homosexual* will enkindle both a definite discomfort with orientation and the desire not to identify with a gay subculture or any gay political agenda. Yet there are many other homosexual persons who believe it is important not to spend energy hiding their homosexuality or trying to "pass" as heterosexuals. Such men and women usually prefer to call themselves gay if male and lesbian if female. Both terms usually reveal a level of comfort and acceptance of a homosexual orientation. Such gay and lesbian persons would most likely share their sexual identities with at least a few chosen relatives and friends. Some others would be totally open about their orientation to everyone in the public arena. Such a posture is often described as "coming out" or "being out of the closet." It is best when dealing with either of these two categories of homosexual people that we use whatever terminology they are comfortable with and use. I believe it is advisable not to assign meanings for words like *gay* or *lesbian* or *homosexual* that may not be intended by the very person that uses these particular terms. Unfortunately, words currently in use have a variety of meanings that involve religious beliefs and nonbeliefs, various agendas and approaches, and some heavily political stances. A good rule of thumb in relating to all homosexual persons is to not make any assumptions. Be welcoming, and as the conversation ensues, various revelations will be shared as a certain level of trust is reached.

"Coming out" or "being out" might also include playing an active role in a certain gay subculture. It sometimes happens that a particular person will choose to live for a time in an all-gay environment. Being part of a gay subculture frequently includes political activism aimed at achieving "gay rights" and a general emancipation of lesbian and gay people. The goals of this activism may include the recognition of "gay marriage" and the acceptance of the belief that a homosexual orientation is equal to and comparable to a heterosexual orientation on every level. Such organized efforts are often referred to as "the gay movement" by some gay people or "the gay agenda" by others who would be opposed to such efforts. Unfortunately, such a gay subculture may be defined by a lifestyle that encompasses anonymous sexual encounters, sex clubs, pornography, drugs and an overidentification with one's homosexual orientation. Such a way of life is sometimes referred to as "the gay lifestyle." The term *gay lifestyle* is unfortunately a generalization often indiscriminately and inaccurately applied to all gay and lesbian people who show any level of comfort in being homosexual persons. Pastoral experience will reveal that there are homosexual Catholics who are comfortable with the reality of their orientation but who in no way approve or enter into what is called "the gay lifestyle." In this book we will use the term *homosexual* as an adjective describing men and women who have a homosexual orientation. I choose to do so for the sake of clarity and simplicity.

What does the church say about being homosexual? The 1986 *Letter to Bishops* clearly teaches:

> Although the particular inclination of the homosexual person is not a sin, it is a more or less strong tendency ordered toward an intrinsic moral evil and thus the inclination itself must be seen as an objective disorder.
>
> Therefore special concern and pastoral attention should be directed toward those who have this condition, lest they be led to believe that the living out of this orientation in homosexual activity is a morally acceptable option. It is not.[4]

Please note the important distinctions this document makes. The orientation itself is not a sin; it is willful and intended genital activity that is a sin. This distinction is often overlooked in our conversations about homosexuality. It is also very important to avoid giving meanings to phrases like "intrinsic moral evil" and "objective disorder" that were never intended. This document is speaking about homosexuality in terms of Catholic morality and Catholic doctrine. This document is not saying that homosexual persons are depraved or that they suffer some mental illness or physical malady. In the pages that follow, I try to clarify such mistaken notions, which can be harmful to homosexual Catholics.

The church has yet more to say. In a 1975 document titled *Persona Humana,* we are taught that some men and women are definitively homosexual because of an innate instinct or constitution, which is incurable (no. 3).[5] So, homosexuality for some people constitutes an innate constitutional fact of their existence. For this reason *Letter to Bishops* asserts that homosexual people are more than their sexual expressions and affirms that "a homosexual person, as every human being, deeply needs to be nourished at many different levels simultaneously."[6] This same document goes on to say clearly:

> The human person, made in the image and likeness of God, can hardly be adequately described by a reductionist reference to his or her sexual orientation. Every one living on the face of the earth has personal problems and difficulties, but challenges to growth, strengths, talents and gifts as well. Today, the Church provides a badly needed context for the care of the human person when she refuses to consider the person as a "heterosexual" or a "homosexual" and insists that every person has a fundamental identity: the creature of God and, by grace, his child and heir to eternal life.[7]

What pastoral conclusions can be drawn from these few Roman Catholic church documents? Sexual orientation *is not only or even primarily a tendency toward genital acts,* but rather a psychosexual, intrapsychic attraction toward particular individual persons. This is to affirm that one's sexual orientation is not fundamentally a tendency toward sexual activity but rather an intrapsychic dimension of one's personality. This broader focus and understanding finds support in "Principles to Guide Confessors in Questions of Homosexuality" in 1973 by the statement that the "deeper need of any human being is for friendship rather than genital expression...."[8]

Many people cannot envision homosexuality as a possibility for authentic love because they regard it simply as a genital, sexual urge or drive. Such persons are misguided. One must remember that anyone's sexual orientation does not simply consist of sexual desire but actually influences the way one thinks, the way one decides, the way one responds, the ways one relates to others—even to God—and the ways one structures his or her world. All those actions that make up each waking moment are shaped by one's sexual orientation.

Father Gerald D. Coleman, S.S., speaks so well to this issue when he says:

> Consequently, the homosexual orientation itself is a manifestation of the capacity and the need of human persons to grow in loving relationships that in some way mirror the life-giving love of the God in whose image and likeness we are all created: i.e., homosexuality is not an orientation to sexual activity as such any more than definitive heterosexuality is. Any sexual activity must be seen in the context of the totality of the persons involved. A homosexual person is not driven in some compulsive manner, as the CDF *Letter* rightly points out (no. 11), to sexual activity: the person is "driven" to experience love, fidelity, meaning, intimacy, in human terms, in terms of relationships that bond individuals to one another in ways that manifest the presence of the God whose love grounds our being.[9]

The church carefully distinguishes between being a homosexual person and acting out in a genital way; these are two separate realities. In making such a distinction, the church also wisely reminds all of us that it is impossible to isolate orientation from the rest of one's life. It is for these reasons that many homosexual persons choose to "come out" at least to some people. When a son or daughter says they are gay or lesbian, they may or may not be wanting to talk about sex. They are more likely wanting to talk about so many other realities in their lives that are shaped by their orientation. This point is alluded to in *Human Sexuality: A Catholic Perspective for Education and Lifelong Learning:*

Sexuality, as noted earlier, is a fundamental dimension of every human being. It is reflected physiologically, psychologically, and relationally in a person's gender identity as well as one's primary sexual orientation and behavior. For some young men and women, this means a discovery that one is homosexual, that is, that one's "sexual inclinations are oriented predominately toward persons of the same sex." Other persons experience a bisexual orientation. These orientations involve one's feelings and sexual fantasies as well as one's overtly sexual and genital actions.[10]

Not a Once-and-for-All Moment

Declaring one's homosexual orientation, or "coming out," is never a once-and-for-all moment. Coming out, once done, is a daily task at work, at play, in church, in school and elsewhere. Homosexual people live much of their existence in a heterosexual world. Heterosexuality is normative and taken for granted. Normally, it is presumed that everyone is heterosexual. Homosexual people are always having to decide if this or that occasion calls for another revelation that they are not heterosexual, but homosexual. And every time one reveals his or her homosexual orientation, there is always a certain risk of rejection, misunderstanding, violence or the loss of a job, a promotion or recognition. Being homosexual is never easy. Part of the complexity of coming out is how such a revelation affects one's parents. How often is it said that when a child comes out of the closet parents go into the closet? "When is your son going to settle down and get married?" is such an innocent and normal question. But if your son is homosexual, the question may be experienced as intrusive and insensitive. A daughter shares an apartment with a woman companion. And years and months pass by and the two companions seem inseparable. How does a parent explain such a relationship to Grandma or Aunt Mildred? It is not easy to come out as a parent. But going through the growing pains of deciding whom to tell and not to tell is often a first step in understanding the courage and the fear of a son or daughter who finally confides his or her secret to a parent.

Self-Awareness

How does one know if she or he is homosexual? If one is male, does he act in an effeminate way? Well, he might, but typically does not. If one is female, does she act a bit masculine? Well, she might, but probably does not. One cannot necessarily discern someone's orientation by something they do or by the way they look or carry themselves. A more important question is how does the homosexual person know or come to such an awareness?

Actually, the process of recognizing and naming oneself homosexual is most commonly a gradual awakening in which the person has to pass through various stages of awareness. I have watched many people go through such a process, and I have listened to many tell their stories of coming to awareness. Typically, a person will likely begin with what could be called a level of attraction. When I am at a party, in a room packed with men and women, whom do I tend to notice without even making a conscious attempt to do so? If a person were a male, he might say: "Why do I always remember the guy's name and cannot remember his girlfriend's name or even remember what she looks like?" If a person were female, she might ask: "Why do I seem to prefer the company of certain women? Why do I have such an intense interest in certain women?" Such experiences constitute one clear sign that may prod me to look more closely at my orientation.

A second level of awareness would be arousal. When I see a particular person of the same sex with a certain body type, build or look, do I note erotic excitement? What types of persons are they? Erotic feelings, even if I do not act on them, are one more sign that I may be homosexual.

Finally, I might arrive at the level of actual experience and reflection on that experience. As I act on my feelings prompted by a kiss, a touch or an embrace, or if I go even farther into some actual genital activity exchange, how do I feel? Feeling here is not merely physical pleasure but a feeling of ease and comfort; this is part of who I am. What shall I do about this? I must make a very careful assessment. Why? Because heterosexual men and women often enough have both males and females in their lives whom they love or for whom they feel some passing attraction. So it is very important to think in terms of how dominant all those feelings around homosexuality are. Many people have an occasional homoerotic thought. But when those feelings are clearly dominant, then I have reasons to believe that I am homosexual. How often I have heard men and women say: "Father, I just know without a doubt who I am."

The above scenario is not meant to indicate that every homosexual person goes through such stages in exactly the same way. There are many ways, situations and occasions that may go into awareness of a homosexual orientation. The examples given above are simply indicators that there is a gradual process of coming to awareness for most homosexual people. In chapter 6 homosexual Catholics will speak of their own experiences and what it means for them to know that they are homosexual. They will speak of their long struggle with assessment, adjustment and integration of that reality in their lives as human beings and Catholic Christians.

A Final Word

Is homosexuality a mental disorder? For many years homosexuality was considered a serious mental disorder. In 1973 the American Psychiatric Association removed homosexuality from the list of mental disorders. In the *Diagnostic and Statistical Manual of Mental Disorders* (3rd ed.) the word *homosexuality* is now replaced by *egodystonic homosexuality*, which the *Manual* describes in the following words:

> The essential features are a desire to acquire or increase heterosexual arousal, so that heterosexual relationships can be initiated or maintained, and a sustained pattern of overt homosexual arousal that the individual explicitly states has been unwanted and a persistent source of distress.[11]

Such persons could understandably need or want to go through psychological counseling to help them with their discomfort. Such a person might also seek out a therapist who will offer reparative therapy as a way of controlling or diminishing the desires of a homosexual orientation or getting over it entirely and realizing a heterosexual orientation.

The *Diagnostic and Statistical Manual of Mental Disorders* also speaks about egosyntonic homosexuality, which simply means that some homosexual persons are not upset by their homosexual orientation and do what they can to accept and integrate their orientation into their lives.

We can conclude this chapter with some good advice from *Always Our Children*. You can help a homosexual person in two general ways. All Catholics are called to live chaste lives. Chastity will vary according to one's state and vocation in life. Yet each one is called to live out the commands of the scriptures and teachings of the church. Homosexual Catholics are no exception and are called to live the chastity of those who are called to the single state. The best way to encourage and support a chaste life is by example. The less effective way is to be stridently objective, not taking into account the spiritual journey of the person you are advising.

"I am the true vine, and my Father is the vine grower." John 15:1

Second, concentrate on the person, not on the homosexual orientation itself. This implies respecting a person's freedom to choose or refuse therapy directed toward changing a homosexual orientation. Given the present state of medical and psychological knowledge, there is no guarantee that such therapy will succeed. Thus there may be no obligation to undertake it, though some find it helpful.[12]

Most importantly, never forget the essential reality that God loves every person. Our sexual identity helps define who we are as persons. Part of sexual identity for some of us is homosexuality. Yet personhood is made up of so much more than one's sexual orientation. We always need to avoid reducing anyone to his or her orientation, heterosexual or homosexual. Finally, you will find nowhere in the scriptures nor in the teachings of our church any support for the opinion that somehow God loves a homosexual person any less than anyone else in the world.

Chapter 3

What Does the Bible Teach?

Does the Bible say anything about homosexuality? Yes, it does, but as we search the Bible, we need a point of reference. That point of reference is the clear teaching of the church. The *Letter to the Bishops of the Catholic Church on the Pastoral Care of Homosexual Persons* places its scriptural understanding of homosexuality within the story of creation in Genesis:

> Human beings, therefore, are nothing less than the work of God himself and in the complementarity of the sexes they are called to reflect the inner unity of the Creator. They do this in a striking way in their cooperation with him in the transmission of life by a mutual donation of the self to the other.
>   …To choose someone of the same sex for one's sexual activity is to annul the rich symbolism and meaning, not to mention the goals, of the Creator's sexual design. Homosexual activity is not a complementary union able to transmit life; and so it thwarts the call to a life of that form of self-giving which the Gospel says is the essence of Christian living.[1]

But something else must also be understood if we are to properly understand what the Bible says about homosexuality. The very notions of *homosexual* and *homosexuality* were simply not known during the times in which the Bible was written. In other words, the Bible most certainly knows about and clearly

27

condemns same-sex genital activity but is completely ignorant of homosexuality as a sexual orientation. Homosexuality as an orientation is a recent and modern-day reality that is studied and debated and researched. The biblical writers simply took for granted that all people were born with a natural attraction to members of the opposite sex; today we would describe such persons as heterosexual. The Bible writers thought of everyone as heterosexual. Let us now examine the biblical texts that address same-sex activity.

Genesis

Genesis 18:20–21 reads: "Then the Lord said: 'The outcry against Sodom and Gomorrah is so great, and their sin so grave, that I must go down and see whether or not their actions fully correspond to the cry against them that comes to me. I mean to find out.'"[2] A most delightful conversation follows between God and Abraham. It is an important point that God is actually ready to destroy Sodom and Gomorrah! But Abraham pleads for mercy: "Will you sweep away the innocent with the guilty?" (v. 23). Abraham asks God to spare the cities if he finds fifty innocent men among the people. God agrees. But Abraham doesn't stop there; he pushes God further until God agrees to spare the cities even if only ten innocent men are found. Then chapter 19 begins:

> The two angels reached Sodom in the evening, as Lot was sitting at the gate of Sodom. When Lot saw them, he got up to greet them; and bowing down with his face to the ground, he said, "Please, gentlemen, come aside into your servant's house for the night, and bathe your feet; you can get up early to continue your journey." But

they replied, "No, we shall pass the night in the town square." He urged them so strongly, however, that they turned aside to his place and entered his house. He prepared a meal for them, baking cakes without leaven, and they dined.

Before they went to bed, all the townsmen of Sodom, both young and old—all the people to the last man—closed in on the house. They called to Lot and said to him, "Where are the men who came to your house tonight? Bring them out to us that we may have intimacies with them." Lot went out to meet them at the entrance. When he had shut the door behind him, he said, "I beg you, my brothers, not to do this wicked thing. I have two daughters who have never had intercourse with men. Let me bring them out to you, and you may do to them as you please. But don't do anything to these men, for you know they have come under the shelter of my roof." They replied, "Stand back! This fellow," they sneered, "came here as an immigrant, and now he dares to give orders! We'll treat you worse then them!" With that, they pressed hard against Lot, moving in closer to break down the door. But his guests put out their hands, pulled Lot inside with them, and closed the door; at the same time they struck the men at the entrance of the house, one and all, with such a blinding light that they were utterly unable to reach the doorway. (Genesis 19:1–11)

After more discussion between the angels and Lot, verses 24–25 and 29 conclude:

…the LORD rained down sulphurous fire upon Sodom and Gomorrah [from the LORD out of heaven]. He overthrew those cities and the whole Plain, together with the inhabitants of the cities and the produce of the soil….Thus it came to pass: when God destroyed the Cities of the Plain, he was mindful of Abraham by sending Lot away from the upheaval by which God overthrew the cities where Lot had been living.

What exactly were the sins of Sodom and Gomorrah? The prophet Jeremiah states that the sins of Sodom were adultery, lying and unrepentance (Jeremiah 23:14). The Book of Ezekiel names Sodom's sins as pride, gluttony, complacency and a refusal to share with the poor, and states that they committed "abominable crimes in [God's] presence...." (Ezekiel 16:49–50). The Book of Wisdom defines the sins of Sodom as folly, insolence and inhospitality (Wisdom 19:13). Jesus refers to Sodom in Luke 10:10 and Matthew 10:14. Here Sodom's sin was inhospitality. Peter 2:4 and Jude 6 offer the suggestion that Sodom's sin was of a sexual nature.

We must conclude that Sodom was involved in numerous sins and offenses against God. Clearly and certainly one of the sins of Sodom was intended homosexual rape. It would be incorrect to conclude that the only sin or the chief sin of Sodom was homosexual intercourse. In the rhetoric and controversy surrounding homosexuality some religious groups do seem to be saying that homosexuality was the only cause of Sodom's destruction. On occasion I have heard a few Catholics speak with the same misunderstanding.

Homosexual genital activity was one among many sins for which scripture condemns Sodom. The Bible is clear: Sexual intercourse is legitimate in Genesis 4 because Adam and Eve were acting in accordance with their married state. However, the same act is an abomination and a sinful act in Genesis 19 because the relationship is not a marital one but one of contemplated homosexual rape.

Leviticus

I am the LORD. You shall not lie with a male as with a woman; such a thing is an abomination. You shall not have carnal relations with an animal, defiling yourself with it; nor shall a woman set herself in front of an animal to mate with it; such things are abhorrent....If a man lies with a male as with a woman, both of them shall be put to death for their abominable deed; they have forfeited their lives. (Leviticus 18:21b–23; 20:13)

The above text from Leviticus is strong and clear. What is permitted between married men and women is not permitted between two men or two women.

1 Timothy

We know that the law is good, provided that one uses it as law, with the understanding that law is meant not for a righteous person but for the lawless and unruly, the godless and sinful, the unholy and profane, those who kill their fathers or mothers, murderers, the unchaste, practicing homosexuals, kidnapers, liars, perjurers, and whatever else is opposed to sound teaching, according to the glorious gospel of the blessed God, with which I have been entrusted. (1 Timothy 1:8–11)

Romans

> While claiming to be wise, they became fools and exchanged the glory of the immortal God for the likeness of an image of mortal man or of birds or of four-legged animals or of snakes.
>
> Therefore God handed them over to impurity through the lusts of their hearts for the mutual degradation of their bodies. They exchanged the truth of God for a lie and revered and worshiped the creature rather than the creator, who is blessed forever. Amen. Therefore, God handed them over to degrading passions. Their females exchanged natural relations for unnatural, and the males likewise gave up natural relations with females and burned with lust for one another. Males did shameful things with males and thus received in their own persons the due penalty for their perversity. (Romans 1:22–27)

In the above passages from the Bible, same-sex genital activity is clearly forbidden. Moreover, the particular passage from Romans 1 is the only reference we have that clearly condemns same-sex activity between women. It is in these words from scripture that the church finds a foundation for its teaching and a belief on the immorality of homosexual genital activity, whether between adult males, or adult males with young boys, or sex between two women. Sometimes the argument is raised that these few passages do not build much of a case against same-sex activity. The response to such an argument is the consistent and high place given to sex within marriage throughout the Old and New Testaments, clearly attesting to the truth that heterosexual marriage is normative and the only legitimate place for all genital activity.

A brief word must be said about the fact that within our

own Catholic Church and outside of it there are voices being raised that challenge the church's understanding and interpretation of the passages from the Bible quoted above. It is not within the scope of this book to treat such new interpretations in any detail. For our purposes here, it will be sufficient to simply recall the church's response to such new interpretations that would result in a change of the teaching of the church on homosexuality. The church does say clearly:

> What should be noticed is that in the presence of such remarkable diversity there is nevertheless a clear consistency with the Scriptures themselves on the moral issue of homosexual behavior. The church's doctrine regarding this issue is thus based not on isolated phrases for facile theological argument, but on the solid foundation of a constant biblical testimony. The community of faith today, in unbroken continuity with the Jewish and Christian communities within which the ancient Scriptures were written, continues to be nourished by those same Scriptures and by the Spirit of truth whose Word they are. It is likewise essential to recognize that the Scriptures are not properly understood when they are interpreted in a way which contradicts the Church's living tradition. To be correct, the interpretation of Scripture must be in substantial accord with that tradition.
>
> The Vatican Council II in *Dei Verbum*, No. 10, put it this way: "It is clear, therefore, that in the supremely wise arrangement of God, sacred tradition, Sacred Scripture and the magisterium of the church are so connected and associated that one of them cannot stand without the others. Working together, each in its own way under the action of the one Holy Spirit, they all contribute effectively to the salvation of souls." In that spirit we wish to outline briefly the biblical teaching here.[3]

A Word of Caution

There are a significant number of Catholics today who are given to a literalist or fundamentalist understanding of the Bible. And it is most unsettling that such literalism is often used when quoting passages from the Bible that have to do with homosexuality. It is certainly clear that the Bible does condemn sexual activity outside of marriage and even more explicitly condemns same-sex activity between two men or two women. But to conclude that the scriptures are the only source of our understanding of homosexuality is to betray the richness of our Catholic tradition. In other words, an approach to homosexuality based on scripture alone is not sufficient and can lead to serious pastoral problems when ministering to homosexual persons or trying to understand the complexity of homosexuality.

We Catholic Christians always speak about scripture and tradition as the two great sources of whatever we believe and teach as the church. Sacred scripture is God's speech put in writing under the breath of the Holy Spirit. Sacred tradition transmits in its entirety God's word. The scriptures alone are never the final word about doctrine and morals. The teachings of the magisterium, the results of research of the natural and social sciences, the lived experience of ordinary faithful Catholics, as well as the insight that comes from prayer and the restlessness of the human heart striving to do the will of God all play a part in how we understand the scriptures and what we are called to believe and teach. To simply quote the Bible and not include these other dimensions is really to lose some of the richness of our Catholic faith. In the next chapter we will complete our examination of the Bible and homosexuality by examining some of the church's magisterial statements on homosexuality.

If the Bible clearly condemns same-sex activity, it even

more roundly condemns hatred, which often finds its expression in injustice and the exclusion of some group or a particular person. And sometimes that prejudice extends itself to a particular sin as being especially evil or destructive of society. Hatred is always wrong and can in no case be justified. It is wrong to single out any group of persons and hate them because of who they are, whether it be a matter of race, nationality, status, sex or sexual orientation. Hatred is wrong whether it is expressed in physical violence, silence or indifference. Hatred is most obvious when connected with the commission of an act, but it can also be very effective by the omission of an act. Hatred is as much about commission as it is about omission. In 1 Corinthians a failure to acknowledge someone in the room with me could be as offensive as offering insulting language. In 1 Corinthians 6:9–10 we read the following poignant words:

> Do you not know that the unjust will not inherit the kingdom of God? Do not be deceived; neither fornicators nor idolaters nor adulterers nor boy prostitutes nor practicing homosexuals nor thieves nor the greedy nor drunkards nor slanderers nor robbers will inherit the kingdom of God.

I would like to point out that in this passage Paul does not single out the homosexual for condemnation. Rather, Paul's list of sins is such that the hearer can easily find himself or herself in a number of categories. We are all sinners. We are all in need of conversion. The minute we point an accusing finger at another, we are really condemning ourselves. It is never helpful nor is it just to single out any homosexual Catholics for judgment or condemnation or to treat them as "especially sinful." And if and when we do so, we really need to examine our motivation for doing so.

Chapter 4

Homosexuality
and Catholic Teaching

What moral judgment does the church bring to homosexual genital activity? The church could not be clearer. All sexual activity outside of marriage is objectively sinful. To begin a chapter with such a statement may appear to be too negative. Why begin there? I do so quite deliberately. Unfortunately, in the mind of many, homosexuality is synonymous with illicit sexual behavior. "Homosexuality is a sin" is a common expression of many religious people. Such a statement presumes that all homosexual persons choose to act out sexually or are compelled to do so and are given to a promiscuous lifestyle of frequent, exploitive sexual encounters. For some people such a misconception is so much taken for granted that if a homosexual person did not act out sexually, they would not think that such a person was homosexual at all or else had been cured. So many parents who come to me are sometimes influenced by such a misconception. They are understandably upset and confused by their child's homosexual orientation. What is heartbreaking to them is an unfounded belief that their children are no longer able to receive holy communion by the simple fact of their orientation. Such parents agonize over the thought that their sons or daughters are in a state of serious sin or are committing sins that will jeopardize their salvation. It is important to allay parents' fears by presenting more accurate information.

Sometimes in sermons and in religious rhetoric, preachers, writers and teachers will list a whole category of sins that plague our society today and are thought to be a serious threat to civilization. Such a list may include artificial birth control, abortion, fornication, adultery, divorce, pedophilia and pornography, just to name a few. It is not uncommon for someone to include homosexuality in such a list of sins. Preachers and teachers will often speak about "the sin of homosexuality." Including homosexuality in a list of sinful actions, without offering explanations and distinctions that are found in church teaching, can be simplistic and misleading. It is for this reason that when some Catholics hear about a ministry to homosexual Catholics, they shake their heads in wonderment. "Are we accepting those people in our church?" "Are we supporting the gay lifestyle?" "What is the Catholic Church coming to." Thus, beginning this chapter with a clear definition of what is sinful and not sinful about homosexuality is an important foundation for understanding and for sound ministry.

In St. Thomas Aquinas's teachings on the gift of sexuality, he makes a distinction between sexual sins "against nature" and sexual sins "according to nature." Sexual sins according to nature are contrary to right reason. Some such sexual sins are fornication, rape, incest and adultery. Sins against nature have an added dimension of not only being contrary to reason but also inconsistent with the very end of sexual activity, which is openness to new human life. Some such sins are masturbation, bestiality, contraception and homosexual intercourse. Such acts, by their very nature, regardless of one's intentions or circumstances, are always forbidden. Another term used for sins that never admit of exceptions is to describe them as "intrinsically evil."

In 1975, the Congregation for the Doctrine of the Faith published a document called *Persona Humana*. The same document is also called The Declaration on Certain Questions Concerning Sexual Ethics. This document teaches that every direct violation of the proper use of sexual activity is objectively a serious sin because the moral order of sexuality always involves values that are important to human life.[1] In his encyclical *The Splendor of Truth*, John Paul II writes clearly on intrinsically sinful acts:

> Reason attests that there are objects of the human act which are by their nature "incapable of being ordered" to God, because they radically contradict the good of the person made in his image. These are the acts which, in the Church's moral tradition, have been termed "intrinsically evil" *(intrinsece malum):* they are such always and per se, in other words on account of their very object and quite apart from the ulterior intentions of the one acting and the circumstances....The Second Vatican Council itself, in discussing the respect due to the human person, gives a number of examples of such acts: "Whatever is hostile to life itself, such as mutilation, physical and mental torture and attempts to coerce the spirit; whatever is offensive to human dignity, such as subhuman living conditions, arbitrary imprisonment, deportation, slavery, prostitution and trafficking in women and children; degrading conditions of work which treat laborers as mere instruments of profit, and not as free responsible persons: all these and the like are a disgrace, and so long as they infect human civilization they contaminate those who inflict them more than those who suffer injustice, and they are a negation of the honor due the Creator.[2]

John Paul II is to be lauded in these few words for his clarity in an area often misused or misunderstood. Hopefully such a list of intrinsically sinful acts may prove helpful and enlightening lest one conclude that same-sex sins are singled out as being uniquely sinful or incomparable with certain other evils.

Principles to Guide Confessors in
Questions of Homosexuality

In 1973 the National Conference of Catholic Bishops pro-
duced *Principles to Guide Confessors in Questions of Homosexuality*.
Principles is primarily addressed to priests and confessors as
guidelines in directing homosexual persons. Yet there is much
that we all can learn from this document.

The first point I would like to take from *Principles* is that
the document states very clearly that the reality of homosexuality
is a highly complex issue that simply does not admit of easy solutions or answers. For this reason the document urges priests to
follow a prudent course when dealing with a homosexual person.
A prudent course judges carefully the subjective culpability of an
individual and thus avoids both harshness and permissiveness.
Principles tells us that a person discovers that he or she is homosexual. One does not choose his or her orientation. "In every case
he *discovers* an already existent condition."[3]

In their document *Human Sexuality*, the bishops of the
United States declare:

> Sexuality, as noted earlier, is a fundamental dimension
> of every human being. It is reflected physiologically,
> psychologically, and relationally in a person's gender
> identity as well as in one's primary sexual orientation
> and behavior. For some young men and women, this
> means a discovery that one is homosexual, that is, that
> one's "sexual inclinations are oriented predominantly
> toward persons of the same sex."[4]

When we say that a person discovers herself or himself to
be homosexual, what is meant? A document of the National

Conference of Catholic Bishops, *Sharing the Light of Faith: National Catechetical Directory for Catholics in the United States,* tells us:

> Sexuality is an important element of human personality, an integral part of one's overall consciousness. It is both a central aspect of one's self-understanding (i.e. as male or female) and a crucial factor in one's relationship with others.[5]

Principles places responsibility on the adult homosexual person to live in accordance with the teaching of the church. Nowhere does the document paint a picture of a homosexual as a driven person incapable of being in command of his or her own life with the assistance of God's grace, in spite of encountering difficulties and challenges:

> It is difficult for the homosexual (person) to remain chaste in his environment, and he may slip into sin for a variety of reasons, including loneliness and compulsive tendencies and the pull of homosexual companions. But, generally, he is responsible for his actions, and the worst thing that a confessor can say is that the homosexual (person) is not responsible for his actions.[6]

Principles goes on to add:

> The priest...should show the person that he can live chastely in the world by means of a plan of life, which will include personal meditative prayer, spiritual reading, reception of the sacraments, and some specific work of charity in the world. Two other elements which should be stressed are regular access to spiritual direction and the formation of a stable friendship with at least one person. One of the greatest difficulties for the homosexual person is the formation of such a friendship.[7]

Make no mistake about it, the above document implies that a homosexual man or woman can enter into a relationship with another homosexual person. Obviously such a relationship is to be platonic or without genital expression. Perhaps such a possibility would come as a surprise to many. Yes, there is a possibility of such chaste unions, and they are desirable because all human beings are made for relationship and have healthy and normal needs for physical touch and affection. In urging the confessor to encourage a homosexual person to enter into a stable relationship with another homosexual person, *Principles* states:

> If a homosexual person has progressed under the direction of a confessor, but in the effort to develop a stable relationship with a given person has occasionally fallen into a sin of impurity, he should be absolved and instructed to take measures to avoid the elements which lead to sin without breaking off a friendship which has helped him grow as a person. If the relationship, however, has reached a stage where the homosexual person is not able to avoid overt actions, he should be admonished to break off the relationship.[8]

If we come out of a rigorist mentality, we might take exception to such a stand as being dangerously permissive. Why would anyone be so foolish as to advise homosexual persons to form intimate relationships? We best recall the church's traditional moral and pastoral teaching regarding what is called the *principle of gradualism.* Conversion is normally not something that happens in an instant or overnight in our Catholic tradition. Conversion is an ongoing process. We grow only gradually. A director must never rush the growth of his penitent. Our movement toward goodness and holiness is a step-by-step process over a period of time. Every confessor and spiritual director must give proper consideration to the disposition and background of the person as well as his understanding and maturity with respect to his faith. The good confessor or director looks at many dimensions and factors so as to help with the discernment of how the Spirit is moving in the life of the one being directed. Authentic ministry can never compromise the church's teaching on human sexuality and the objective sinfulness of homosexual activity. At the same time, such ministry can never happen at the expense of the principle of gradualism.

It is important to realize in general that homosexual persons, like all human persons, seek out deep relationships with other homosexual persons because of the universal need for intimacy. The church clearly teaches that any genital expression in such intimate relationships is immoral. The principle of gradualism recognizes sinfulness where it exists but stresses that genuine growth and conversion from sin comes about not in an instant but over a period of time. The principle of gradualism assumes that a person is striving to incorprate in one's life the biblical and magisterial teaching. Who of us does not battle daily with personal sinfulness and limitations? Who would deprive a homosexual person of the same struggle? Not taking the principle of gradualism into consideration can lead to a kind of self-styled holiness and perfectionism that makes us strangers to God's mercy and forgiveness. Such perfectionism easily turns into self-righteousness, which is a doorway to harsh and condemning judgments of self and others.

To Live in Christ Jesus

In 1976 the National Conference of Catholic Bishops wrote a pastoral letter called *To Live in Christ Jesus: A Pastoral Reflection on the Moral Life.* That document wisely teaches that moral teaching is not some external and foreign command imposed on us from on high, but is really an expression of the human person restored in Christ. It was with such a truth in mind that the bishops wrote the following words:

> Some persons find themselves through no fault of their own to have a homosexual orientation. Homosexuals, like everyone else, should not suffer from prejudice against their basic human rights. They have a right to respect, friendship, and justice. They should have an active role in the Christian community. Homosexual activity, however, as distinguished from homosexual orientation, is morally wrong. Like heterosexual persons, homosexuals are called to give witness to chastity, avoiding, with God's grace, behavior that is wrong for them, just as nonmarried sexual relations are wrong for heterosexuals. Nonetheless, because heterosexuals can usually look forward to marriage, and homosexuals, while their orientation continues, might not, the Christian community should provide them a special degree of pastoral understanding and care.[9]

What can we conclude from these words? Homosexuality is not chosen; it is an orientation that is discovered. It is always inappropriate to demonstrate or express in word or deed any kind of prejudice against a homosexual person. Respect, friendship and justice are rights that belong to all human beings, including homosexual Catholics, by reason of their baptism, which no one can take from them. They enjoy all the rights and responsibilities belonging to all the members of the church.

To Live in Christ Jesus also calls homosexual persons to the same chaste life to which all members of the church are called. Chastity for all believers is not simply abstinence from all illicit activity. Chastity also has to do with positive values such as modesty in words, deeds and actions. Chastity offers resistance to lustful desires and temptations and any practice that abuses the meaning of sexuality. Chastity also encourages social and legal policy that would defend and support the sacredness of human sexuality. Chastity is about self-control and responding to graces given to live a chaste life. Everyone is called to chastity according to his or her state in life.

Letter to the Bishops of the Catholic Church on the Pastoral Care of Homosexual Persons

Letter to Bishops was written in 1986. The letter goes to great pains to clarify the church's position on homosexuality. The reason for such clarifications was a reaction to certain more liberal notions advocated in the public debate on homosexuality. It was felt that a more permissive attitude toward homosexuality found in society was also influencing members of the church. *Letter to Bishops* defends against what it sees as too benign an interpretation of the homosexual orientation, as if it were some good in itself. In the same letter there is a defense made against militant groups who pressure the church to change its teachings or to adopt newer interpretations of those passages in the Bible that condemn homosexual activity.

The pastoral letter cautions against a simplistic and universal condemnation of homosexual persons who act out in sexual activity. As the 1975 *Declaration* of the Congregation for the Doctrine of the Faith puts it: "…homosexuals must certainly be treated with understanding and sustained in the hope of overcoming their personal difficulties.…Their culpability will be judged with prudence."[10] The *Letter to Bishops* clearly concludes "…the particular inclination of the homosexual person is not a sin...."[11] In the same paragraph, *Letter* adds words that are certainly doctrinally correct but that have been a cause for hurt and much heated debate. At times one might think that these were the only message of *Letter*. Those words are as follows:

> Although the particular inclination of the homosexual person is not a sin, it is a more or less strong tendency ordered toward an intrinsic moral evil and thus the inclination itself must be seen as an objective disorder.[12]

This particular passage can be confusing to homosexual persons and to those who minister to them. There are those who confuse this statement with the notion that homosexual orientation is a mental disorder. Nothing of the kind is indicated here. Some interpret this passage as indicating that a homosexual person is disordered. Some also interpret this section to mean that the orientation is sinful. It is not! Perhaps the simplistic explanation is this: Sexuality is ordered toward procreation and the complementarity between the sexes. If this is how sexuality is ordered, then any action or inclination directed otherwise is considered to be objectively disordered. The word *objective* tells us that we are not speaking about the person (subjective) but of the inclination itself, apart from the person. Perhaps the best explanation of what is intended is found in the often quoted words of Archbishop Quinn:

> This is philosophical language. The inclination is a disorder because it is directed to an object that is disordered. The inclination and the object are in the same order philosophically....In trying to understand this affirmation, we should advert to two things. First, every person has disordered inclinations, for instance, the inclination to rash judgment is disordered, the inclination toward cowardice, the inclination to

hypocrisy, these are all disordered inclinations. Consequently, homosexual persons are not the only ones who have disordered inclinations. Second, the letter does not say that the homosexual person is disordered. Speaking of the homosexual person, the letter states that the Church "refuses to consider the person as a 'heterosexual' or 'homosexual' and insists that every person has a fundamental identity: a creature of God and, by grace, His child and heir to eternal life…." Consequently, the document affirms the spiritual and human dignity of the homosexual person while placing a negative moral judgment on homosexual acts and a negative philosophical judgment on the homosexual inclination or orientation, which it clearly states is not a sin or moral evil.[13]

I would only add a further comment on Archbishop Quinn's remarks. The use of philosophical language does not lead one to conclude that a homosexual orientation is a sickness, a mental disturbance or perversion, or a sin. And how then shall we regard a particular homosexual person if he or she is sexually active? Nothing in our Catholic tradition allows us to make generalizations when assessing individual cases.

> Circumstances may exist, or may have existed in the past, which would reduce or remove the culpability of the individual in a given instance: or other circumstances may increase it. What is at all costs to be avoided is the unfounded and demeaning assumption that the sexual behavior of homosexual persons is always and totally compulsive and therefore inculpable. What is essential is that the fundamental liberty, which characterizes the human person, and gives him his dignity may be recognized as belonging to the homosexual person as well. As in every conversion

from evil, the abandonment of homosexual activity will require a profound collaboration of the individual with God's liberating grace.[14]

Archbishop Quinn maintains that in same-sex activity culpability is not always easy to determine. We must be careful of our judgment. To view the sexual behavior of a homosexual person as always compulsive and inculpable is both demeaning and unfounded. The fundamental liberty that is part of every human person also belongs to homosexual persons. Finally, it should be obvious that homosexuality is a variation in human orientation. We will speak more about this in a later chapter on the origins of homosexuality.

The *Catechism*

I wish to conclude this chapter by quoting completely the entire section of the *Catechism of the Catholic Church* in its treatment of homosexuality.

Homosexuality refers to relations between men or between women who experience an exclusive or predominant sexual attraction toward persons of the same sex. It has taken a great variety of forms through the centuries and in different cultures. Its psychological genesis remains largely unexplained. Basing itself on Sacred Scripture, which presents homosexual acts as acts of grave depravity, tradition has always declared that homosexual acts are "intrinsically disordered." …They do not proceed from a genuine affective and sexual complementarity. Under no circumstances can they be approved.

The number of men and women who have deep-seated homosexual tendencies is not negligible. This inclination, which is objectively disordered, constitutes for most of them a trial. They must be accepted with respect, compassion, and sensitivity. Every sign of unjust discrimination in their regard should be avoided. These persons are called to fulfill God's will in their lives and, if they are Christians, to unite to the sacrifice of the Lord's Cross the difficulties they may encounter from their condition.

Homosexual persons are called to chastity. By the virtues of self-mastery that teach them inner freedom, at times by the support of disinterested friendship, by prayer and sacramental grace, they can and should gradually and resolutely approach Christian perfection.[15]

These three brief paragraphs are a summary of the many documents that have been written on homosexuality. If I were to put the *Catechism* in a narrative form, it might read as follows:

To experience an exclusive or predominant sexual attraction to members of the same sex is part of what it means to be homosexual. This reality appears in every age and culture. Its origin remains as much a mystery as the reality itself. In searching the scriptures for some direction and meaning, it is clear that sexual practices find their true meaning within the context of the sacrament of matrimony. But even in marriage, such practices are ordered toward openness to the possibility of new life and expressive of a complementarity between the sexes. All other sexual activity outside of marriage is therefore disordered and objectively sinful. Given the hardships that accompany a homosexual orientation, all members of the church are called to be supportive and understanding, offering homosexual persons respect, compassion and sensitivity. And the church must also guard against any unjust discrimination against homosexual persons. Homosexual persons, like all members of the church, are called to live chastely according to their state in life. And like all the baptized, fortified by prayer and the grace of the sacraments, they are able to live fully the call to discipleship. The orientation itself is a trial for most, because it normally separates them from the possibility of marriage, children and so many other blessings the majority may take for granted. Yet, it is that cross of suffering and separateness that often becomes the source of a virtuous life of compassion and solidarity with the outsider and the alien. Their number is not negligible, and they are capable of living holy and exemplary lives in the service of the church.

"I will give you a new heart and place a new spirit within you, taking from your bodies your stony hearts and giving you natural hearts."
Ezekiel 36:26

Chapter 5

The Origins of Homosexuality

I have yet to meet a person who claimed to have chosen to be homosexual. In listening to homosexual men and women speak to their lived experience, the vast majority have spent considerable time and effort doing everything possible to rid themselves of their homosexual tendencies, feelings and attractions. Such efforts range from sincere prayer to God for deliverance to an elaborate system of hiding true feelings and acting "straight" with the hope that all tendencies toward the same sex will one day just disappear like a bad dream. Sad to say, too many homosexual persons attempt marriage and even parenting, not to deceive their spouses, whom they often love deeply, but with a hope that a milieu of normalcy will lead them to a more peaceful existence, with all the benefits, securities and blessings of family, church and society. Many such persons spend years in therapy and counseling. "Father, if homosexuality were truly a choice, there would be no homosexuals in this world." I have heard those words hundred of times.

The reality of homosexuality stares us in the face more than at any other time in history. Homosexuality is not new. What is new is that it is out in the open now. We talk about it. We try to make some sense out of it. The energy it takes to hide and pretend is too costly: ruined marriages, disrupted parent-child relationships, double lives of secrecy, internal conflicts and isolation. Many choose to live in denial of their homosexuality. No doubt some of the strong reactions toward even a discussion of homosexuality have to do with denial of one kind or another. But we must deal with it as best we can. One way to deal with it is by trying to understand the origins of homosexuality. Where does it come from? How do those I love and care about get this way?

In spite of much research and the proposal of many theories and hypotheses, little is known or understood about homosexuality with any kind of absolute certitude. We are still only at the beginning stages of understanding. Adding to the confusion is the politicizing of this or that theory. And when you think about it, how much do we know about the origins of heterosexuality? This is a scary question. What is normative is taken for granted. And while such a question does not carry the same urgency that homosexuality does, it certainly is a sobering and humbling question. There is much to learn about human sexuality.

The social sciences have presented various theories to explain sexual orientation, but no theory has been conclusively proven to be true. One of the problems is that there is no one way that all homosexual men and women feel and act. Such a variety of experience and expression could easily point to the fact that there may well be a number of homosexualities. If there are many homosexualities, perhaps there are a number of ways people become homosexual.

As recently as 1990, *The Kinsey Institute Report on Sex* told us that no one knows what causes homosexuality. The report says:

> Many theories have been proposed, but so far most have not held up under careful scrutiny and none have been proven. In fact, scientists probably have a clearer idea of what does "not" cause a homosexual orientation. Children raised by gay or lesbian parents or couples, for instance, are *no* more likely to grow up to be homosexual than are children raised by heterosexual parents....

It also is not true that people become homosexuals because they were seduced by an older person of the same sex in their youth. The childhood and adolescent sexual experiences of both homosexuals and heterosexuals recall later that they found opposite-sex encounters less satisfying than did heterosexuals.

Current theory is that there probably are many different developmental paths by which a person can come to be homosexual, bisexual or heterosexual.[1]

In 1986, the Kinsey Institute held a symposium for researchers representing various disciplines, including sociology, psychiatry, medicine, history, biology, psychology and anthropology. The purpose of the symposium was to reexamine previous findings. The conclusions are enlightening. It is taken for granted that sexual experience is what makes one homosexual. Many Catholic people continue to believe this myth. But it seems that homosexuality has other indicators and factors, that is, love, sexual attraction, fantasy and self-identification. And adding to the complexity of the findings of the Kinsey Institute is the fact that these factors can change over a period of time. So, once again, according to the Kinsey Institute, there probably are a number of *homosexualities* that can be noted among homosexual men and women. In other words, according to this report, it would seem more accurate to say that homosexual orientation is multidimensional, situational and contextual. Homosexuality is comprised of a variety of experiences and expressions. And what practical conclusion may we draw here? It would seem that speaking about *the homosexual lifestyle* is misleading and an inaccurate generalization that is not justified.

You may be familiar with a perennial question that is still popular. Is homosexuality the result of nurturing or the result of nature. Is homosexuality the result of biology or environment? One can find researchers who claim that homosexuality can be traced to family upbringing, particularly a child's relationship with his or her parents. Other researchers speak of physical causes, such as the structure of the brain or hormonal exposure in the embryonic state of development. Most recently and significantly, there has been research that indicates differences in the brains of heterosexual men that supports the theory that homosexuality has a biological foundation.

It must be remembered that in the 1880s homosexuality was commonly viewed as a sickness. Vestiges of such a theory are very much alive among a number of people today. Obviously such a view invited a cure on the part of many doctors. Attempted treatments in years past were rather drastic and included castration, hypnosis, electric shock, hysterectomies, and later, psychoanalysis.

Why would any such theory or scientific research hold any interest for Catholics dealing with homosexuality? If homosexuality is wrong, would it not make sense to understand homosexuality as an illness? I do not think so. Vatican II's Pastoral Constitution on the Church in the Modern World *(Gaudium et Spes)* states that:

> The recent studies and findings of science, history and philosophy raise new questions which effect life and which demand new theological investigations. Furthermore, theologians, within the requirements and methods proper to theology, are invited to seek continually for more suitable ways of communicating doctrine to the men of their times; for the deposit of Faith or the truths are one thing and the manner in which they are enunciated, in the same meaning and understanding, is another. In pastoral care, sufficient use must be made not only of theological principles, but also of the findings of the secular sciences, especially of psychology and sociology, so that the faithful

may be brought to a more adequate and mature life of faith.[2]

One of the riches of our Catholic heritage is that we are open to truth wherever it may be found. Truth is one. What science discovers is not automatically opposed to the truths of faith and morals, but often offers helpful insights that assist our life of faith. Certainly this would be true in the complex issue of homosexuality. And precisely because of our openness to what the sciences tell us, the Catholic position on homosexuality often differs from other Christian traditions that may take either a more liberal attitude or too harsh an attitude in their response to homosexuality.

So, from a scientific point of view, the origins of homosexuality are to be found in genetics, prenatal/hormonal, adult postnatal/hormonal and psychological factors. We will touch on some of the conclusions that derive from such research. However, in a modest book of this nature, such academic and detailed technical information is really beyond our scope and intent. For such detail, and totally from a Catholic perspective, I highly recommend Father Gerald D. Coleman's book, *Homosexuality, Catholic Teaching and Pastoral Practice.*[3]

Evidence from the Sciences

In 1991 Simon Le Vay, a biologist, discovered that among homosexual men who died of HIV/AIDS, part of the anterior hypothalamus, an area of the brain that governs sexual behavior, has the form usually found in women rather than the form found in heterosexual men. Such evidence, though not conclusive, is some indication that such a difference may be one cause of homosexuality in men.[4] Neuroscientist Sandra Witelson reports that evidence from anatomical, genetic, hormonal and neuropsychological research is converging to suggest that sexual orientation may well be part of a larger constellation of cognitive attributes. Such research may explain why homosexual men have abilities as well as attractions geared toward certain professions usually ignored by their heterosexual counterparts. What is significant, according to Witelson, is that several independent studies have clearly shown that various brain structures differ among people of differing sexual orientations.[5] The scientific research of Michael Bailey of Northwestern University and Richard Pillard of Boston University of Medicine also offer clear evidence that male sexual orientation is substantially genetic.[6] In July 1993, a team of National Institutes of Health scientists published a most significant study in *Science,* claiming that they have identified a small stretch of genetic material that is linked to male homosexuality. Chandler Burr, a journalist writing on biology and homosexuality concludes:

> The evidence, although preliminary, strongly indicates a genetic and biological basis for all sexual orientation. We see this in the work of scientists Michael Bailey and Richard Pillard, who have done studies on twins and gay and lesbian siblings. For example, they found that with identical twins, where one twin is gay, the other twin has an approximately 50% chance of being gay. In fraternal twins (separate eggs), if one sibling is gay, there is a 16% chance the other sibling will be gay. And in nongenetically related adopted brothers and sisters, when one sibling will be homosexual, it is approximately the normal statistical incidence in the general population. These results, which indicate that sexual orientation is governed primarily by genetics, have been confirmed dramatically in other laboratories in the United States.[7]

You may have heard of the *psychoanalytic theory* as one way of explaining homosexual orientation. I touch on it here because this particular theory is made much of these days by the religious right as well as persons from the political right, in addition to very sincere and caring people who might be of a very conservative mind. Because such an approach may offer relief from the tendency toward homosexual attractions and feelings or raise hope for a complete change from homosexuality to heterosexuality or a way out of the *gay lifestyle,* it is understandable that such a theory would be attractive to a homosexual person whose sexual orientation brings with it terrible pain and emotional distress. It is also understandable that such an approach would be most appealing to parents who are particularly distraught at the news that their sons or daughters are homosexual. Pastors, religion teachers, youth directors and many others could easily entertain such a theory. Should we not look for a way out of a situation that may lead to sin? Should we not do all we can to relieve the pain and doubt that comes with homosexuality? Should we not open every door that may lead to what is normal and healthy? Of course! Yet, I would urge great caution and reserve. Examine the facts carefully and thoughtfully. Think of the implications. What are the risks? Is such an approach endorsed or encouraged by the church?

What does the psychoanalytic theory say about the origins of homosexuality? Homosexuality is due to a disturbance in the parent-child relationship. A boy, for example, could have a distant and cold father and a smothering and controlling mother. The results could easily be that the boy seeks the company and comfort of another male and at the same time fears that relationship as something beyond his reach. This same dynamic can happen with a girl who might be homosexual. Such children, unless there is some kind of psychological intervention, will spend their lives looking for something among members of their own sex that can only be found in a male-female heterosexual relationship.

There is another possibility in the psychoanalytic theory. I call it the *learning theory*. If a male child's first sexual experience was molestation by a favorite and trusted uncle and the boy had already exhibited effeminate behavior that could be interpreted as a predisposition for homosexuality, it is not unreasonable to conclude that such an experience could lead him to be homosexual in his adult life.

In both cases above, the assumption is that the child has learned to be homosexual. The obvious assumption is: *That which has been learned, can be unlearned.* The process of unlearning obviously would involve long-term therapy, which often goes by the name *reparative therapy*.

What are we to make of such an approach? Researchers Bell, Weinberg and Hammersmith questioned 997 homosexual people and 477 heterosexual persons, a representative and matched sample of the total population. Their study took ten years to complete. One of their findings is most helpful to us here.

> For the benefit of readers who are concerned about what parents may do to influence their children's sexual preference, we would restate our findings in another way. No particular phenomenon of family life can be singled out, on the basis of findings as especially consequential for either homosexual or heterosexual development. You may supply your sons with footballs and your daughters with dolls, but no one can guarantee that they will enjoy them. What we have seemed to have identified…is a pattern of feelings and reactions within the child that cannot be traced back to a single social or sociological root; indeed, homosexuality may arise from a biological precursor (e.g., as do left-handedness and allergies) that parents cannot control. In short, to concerned parents, we cannot recommend anything beyond care, sympa-

thy and devotion that good parents presumably lavish on all their children anyway.[8]

Some Conclusions

There is a general agreement today among specialists that no one theory can explain homosexuality. There is much evidence that there are a number of factors that lead to a homosexual orientation for some people, and it is likely that those factors are different for each person. In spite of much research, homosexuality remains a most complex reality. Even church documents make frequent use of the word *complex* when speaking about homosexuality. We therefore need to be cautious with fast and hard answers about homosexuality at this time.

How shall we respond to change therapies and conversion techniques and religious programs that promise to alleviate homosexual feelings and inclinations or even cure persons of their homosexuality? Read their literature and brochures carefully. Such programs normally require tremendous effort on the part of the subject. Success rates are never earthshaking. How much follow-up is done to prove that claims of change or cure are enduring realities? Such programs are normally very expensive. One wonders if it is appropriate to make *change of orientation* such a concentrated focus of one's life. Who reduces life to dealing with his or her orientation? I believe that our church is rich in some typically Catholic treasures. Our spirituality tends to be where we find, through grace, prayer, sacraments, etc., *a way through* certain situations. We do not normally find a way out of situations. We know and believe as much as anyone that God can be found in the light. But we have a long tradition that tells us that we can find God in the darkness as well. In that same tradition, we speak of moments of desolation and consolation. There is the cross and the crown. There is death and there is resurrection. In other words, God can also be found in unresolved conflicts and struggles. God is found as much in the darkness as in the light.

Ex-gay ministries, sponsored by religious groups, are often from a fundamentalist tradition. Close association with such groups leaves a door open to biblical fundamentalism, which tends to take the scriptures in a purely literal sense. Fundamentalism would view the Bible as a kind of map or guide, containing all the answers to our spiritual questions and problems. Each word and phrase is sacred. Such thought is not only foreign to our Catholic tradition, but undermines the very richness of how Catholics read and interpret the Bible. When the scriptures are proclaimed in the church, their proclamation becomes an encounter with God and his Son Jesus Christ. And gathered around that Word, we are instructed in the ways of discipleship. We can never exhaust the depths of Jesus' teaching or how it is to shape our lives and the events of our lives. So it is, that at the end of the reading we make this acclamation: *"The Word of the Lord."* We do not say, *"This is the Word of the Lord."* The omission of the words "This is" makes all the difference in the world. And finally, in our Catholic tradition, scripture can never be the only source of faith or the only meaning of all we believe and teach about homosexuality and everything else. A second source is Tradition. Tradition transmits in its entirety the Word of God, which has been entrusted to the apostles and their successors so that they may preserve and expound the teachings of the Bible. Scripture and Tradition must be honored and accepted with equal sentiments of devotion and reverence.

There is one other difference between our Catholic viewpoint and fundamentalism. We are a church of sacraments. Sacraments are not things; they are celebrations of the presence of the risen Lord in the midst of the church. These sacred moments of encounter are the chief means of any Catholic's conversion. Such a notion is foreign to fundamentalism, whose focus is only on prayer, the laying on of hands and counseling. The central place given to the sacraments is depreciated, particularly the sacrament of reconciliation and Eucharist, with an unguarded association with fundamentalism.

Having dealt so long with homosexual Catholics who have attempted marriages that end in broken hearts and annulments, I shudder at the thought that some of the so-called ex-gays now enter into marriage, claiming that are now *"straight," as God has created everyone to be.* I do not believe that the sacrament of marriage should be a testing ground for highly controversial and questionable theories. And certainly, a good Catholic guideline to be followed is this: There is absolutely nothing in any of the church's documents that supports or hints at the requirement of a homosexual man or woman to change their orientation from homosexual to heterosexual. It is one thing to respect and support a homosexual who might want to take such a course. It is a whole other story to bring pressure to bear on the church to adopt such a policy or to assume that this is the approach the church should take. I deal daily with homosexual people who courageously live deeply committed and holy lives. They live daily with their homosexual orientation. How do they manage? How do they survive? The answers to these questions will be found in the next chapter, which contains the witness of some ordinary homosexual Catholic men and women whose lives and struggles bear a beautiful and powerful witness to the power of God working in their lives.

Chapter 6

I Choose to Stay in the Church

The Book of Ruth, which can be found in the Old Testament, is a charming story that can be read in just a few minutes. The Book of Ruth is named after the Moabite woman who entered into God's people through her marriage with Boaz of Bethlehem.

The book extols filial piety as something that God rewards, even when practiced by a stranger. God favored Ruth's piety, her spirit of self-sacrifice and her moral integrity with the gift of faith and an illustrious marriage through which she became the ancestress of David and of Christ. In this little story the universality of the messianic reign is foreshadowed. All are welcome. Even if you have never read the Book of Ruth, the following words of Ruth to Naomi are familiar to most everyone:

> But Ruth said, "Do not ask me to abandon or forsake you! For wherever you go I will go, wherever you lodge I will lodge, your people shall be my people, and your God my God. Wherever you die I will die, and there be buried. May the LORD do so and so to me, and more besides if aught but death separates me from you! (Ruth 1:16–17)

I chose these words of Ruth because they recall for me the sentiments and convictions of those homosexual Catholic men and women who remain faithful members of the church in spite of so many obstacles. Why do some remain so steadfast in the faith? Why do so many abandon the church?

A good place to look for answers to such questions is the experience of what it is like to be homosexual. Andrew Sullivan is a writer and a homosexual Catholic. He has a reputation for pushing for a change in the church's teaching. But when he speaks of his own journey as a homosexually oriented person, he articulates eloquently some of the pain and quandaries that are his but are equally part of the experience of many other Catholic homosexual people. He writes:

> The secret, then, began when I was young. I hardly dared mention it to anyone; and the complete absence of any note of the subject in my family or in my school, in television, newspapers, or even such books as I could get hold of, made the secret that much more mystifying. I wondered whether there was any physical manifestation of this unmentionable fact. I was circumcised, unlike many other English boys: had that done it? I remember looking up physical descriptions of men and women in the local library to see if my own body corresponded to the shape of the male (I was, I determined, not broad-shouldered enough). When I was a little late through puberty, I wondered whether that might be related, and half imagined that my voice might not break, and reveal my difference. Eventually, I succumbed to panic and mentioned it before God. I was in the communion line at my local parish church, Our Lady and Saint Peter's, the church that was linked to my elementary school. Please, I remember asking the Almighty almost offhandedly as I walked up the aisle to receive communion from the mild-mannered Father Simmons for the umpteenth time, please, help me with *that*.[1]

The one word that stands out in Andrew Sullivan's words is *different*. I most often hear homosexual Catholics saying: "Father,

I just always knew I was different." And *different* is an excellent word to describe how and where one stands in relation to family, work, health and safety, the church and society.

Family

So much of our sense of belonging depends on our relationship with our immediate family, with our family of origin. And in our Catholic Church, we speak so strongly about the importance of the family and the support it deserves. I have met many good families who are able to be loving and accepting of their homosexual sons and daughters. And I am also aware of families who simply cut off a son or daughter who is homosexual. Others might not go so far, provided that the son or daughter keeps their orientation hidden. Demanding hiddenness and secrecy is really a type of rejection. It must be mentioned that the homosexual person is also going to have to forfeit family life with a spouse, children, grandchildren and so many other blessings that most people may take for granted.

Work

Being homosexual, for some, can be so devastating that they never really measure up to their full potential in their professional lives. Some become overachievers who have unreasonable expectations of themselves, which can lead to poor health. Still others fear exposure and prejudice, which are well etched in their memories and experiences.

Health and Safety

Violence against homosexual men and women is well known. Yet, what is reported is hardly commensurate with reality, because many such crimes go unreported for obvious reasons. The 1999 brutal murder of Matthew Shepard is a dramatic sign of the internalized rage and hatred that lies in the hearts of many people. HIV and AIDS have brought tremendous losses that call for a state of grief. Physical and mental health issues are always problematic when people are shamed, persecuted or excluded. Negativity, especially if it originates from our relationship with important personages in our lives, is easily internalized and then acted out in destructive ways.

Religion

I have found no lack of spirituality or faith among homosexual people. But that religiosity is not often exercised in an institutional church. There is no question that there is a good deal of enmity felt by many homosexuals and directed toward established religion. The church is experienced as judgmental, making demands on them that would not be made of any other segment of the church, and, at the same time, generally removed and aloof from their plight. What is particularly disheartening is the number of homosexual former Catholics who have joined other more liberal faith communities.

Society

Many homosexual people simply feel left out of mainstream life. That sense of total alienation finds its fullest expression in what could be called the gay ghettos in most major cities. Los Angeles has its West Hollywood and San Francisco has its Castro. Such communities attract some people who are really on the fringe of society and who exhibit an in-your-face attitude and bizarre behavior and dress that are meant to draw negative attention and are so often exploited by the media. At their worst, such places are the gathering of persons around their brokenness. At their best, such places provide a temporary refuge for people who have nowhere else to go or who just need to be with other homosexual people for entertainment and a sense of community. I have become accustomed to seeing such a neighborhood as the marketplace where evangelization is waiting to happen. My attitude has led me to find goodness and light there as well. What is important to realize is that such places speak clearly to the fact that all human beings are called to relationship and community by their very nature. Exclude any group of people from traditional communities and they will establish their own communities as a means of survival.

If the above information seems too theoretical, some stories and accounts of real people may be helpful. I have changed names and places for the sake of confidentiality. I have changed some of the material for the sake of clarity. The sum and substance of each story is true.

Paraphrases of personal stories with author response

Look and Listen First

My name is Pablo. I have lived this life for fifty-four years. After reflection and prayer, however, it occurred to me that what I really would have wanted to say to the church for a long time is very simple. Perhaps the words of Will Rogers say it best for me:

> An Indian always looks back after he passes something so he can get a view of it from both sides. A white man doesn't do that. He just figures that all sides of a thing are automatically the same. That is why you should never judge a man while you are facing him. You should go around behind him like an Indian and look at what he is looking at, then go back and face him and you will have a totally different idea of who he is.

What I am here to say to the church is that you should go around behind like an Indian and look and learn. Learn what the lives of your lesbian sisters and gay brothers are all about from their side. Ask us what it is like to walk in our shoes. Look and listen before you judge and speak.

My life is only one life, one story of an experience of being gay and called to faith. Over the years, I have heard the stories of many others that are on the same path as I. What I share, I believe, represents the experience of many, at least many of my generation.

I have created a list of words and impressions that I hope convey my point. First of all, the gay experience is the experience of being *different*. I do not remember a time when I did not know it. Long before I was sexual, I was different.

The gay experience is somehow the experience of being *bad*. The topic, if discussed at all, is discussed in hushed tones so the children will never hear. No mention is made of history's heroes who happen to be homosexual. No role models of gay discipleship are ever presented. And always, the whole experience is reduced to genital acts.

The gay experience is the experience of *secrecy*. If you are homosexual, keep it to yourself. Keep it quiet. Keep it in the closet. Keep it from Mom and Dad. Become two people. Live in two worlds. Anyway, if they find out, they will not want me. People will not employ me. People will not befriend me. And who wants to be called a fag anyway?

The gay experience is the experience of *loneliness*. The problem goes beyond sex. The real challenge is intimacy, self-disclosure, acceptance and love.

I gave you the negatives first. Allow me to speak about some positive aspects of being gay. The gay experience is the experience of *freedom:* a freedom from rigid definitions of manliness and womanliness, a freedom that blossoms into tremendous creativity.

The gay experience is the experience of *compassion*. How could a people who have experienced so much exclusion not become experts in inclusion? It was not until years later that I understood what had moved us to march with Martin Luther King or to protest with Caesar Chavez. We know the pain that those brothers and sisters longed to end.

The gay experience is an experience opened to the call of *discipleship*. The Lord who is with those whom others branded as sinners and treated as outcasts has found many listeners among lesbian and gay people. The love of Christ compels us to love in response.

These thoughts of mine are in no way conclusions; they are meant only as sentences in a conversation with our sisters and brothers in faith. Come to the conversation ready to listen to the stories. I know that in your parishes, schools and families, there are gay and lesbian persons waiting to begin this conversation with you. We wait to sense that the church has gone behind to look, to listen, to learn and to deepen its understanding of the world as experienced by its gay and lesbian disciples. Thank you.

◈ *A Personal Response*

I offer these few comments. Each person's life is the sacred arena of the action and presence of God. In our ordinary routines, in our goodness and in our badness, in our joys and in our sorrows, in our failures and in our successes, God reveals himself to us as healing, reconciling, nourishing and teaching.

To invite another to tell his or her story is a first mark of welcome. Such an account of the intimate moments of another's life is always a precious gift to be received with reverence and respect. Certainly there are people who are naturally gifted with the gift of listening. There are also those who are professionally trained to listen. I believe that all of us, if we relate to persons, need to learn and develop the art of listening. I would like to offer a few guidelines that may help one to listen more effectively. Respect does not mean being less than honest and candid with the speaker. We may disagree. We may raise questions. We may express disagreement. But to fail to listen or to have an attitude that the stories of others are not worth telling is a serious mistake that may set the groundwork for despair and self-loathing. Being invited to hear another's story is an act of trust that requires not a little courage. Ultimately it can be a moment of saving grace for the teller and the hearer.

Called to Be Mother and Grandmother

By the common baptism we share, I journey with you. I too have my story to tell. Yes, I am a lesbian woman. I am also a mother of three adult children whom I raised as a single parent. The joy of my life is my grandson. He and his mother live with me while my daughter completes her education. I also have a professional life. I am a nurse who works with the terminally ill. I have other involvements in civic and philanthropic groups. Why share all of this? I am telling you that I am more like you than different. When I decided to come out, who was the most difficult person to tell? Myself! It took many years of therapy before I could admit to myself who I was. When I was able to share the news with my daughters, they said they had figured that out long ago. I was out. I could never go back into the closet. But who was I now?

Well, I know I am a homosexual. I did not become homosexual. I believe I have been so from the moment of my conception. I like myself the way I am. I am an active member of my parish. Everyone knows me and they know what I am. I try to be conscious of the fact that I am not only a lesbian; I am a child of God. Because I am out of my closet now, I am a better Catholic Christian today. I can stand before the church and say: I am a mother. I am a grandmother. I am a daughter, a sister, a nurse, a friend and above all else, I am always thanking God for all his graces and enrichments.

A Personal Response

If the climate had been more accepting and understanding of homosexuality, the woman in this story would not have tried to hide in marriage. There would not have been an annulment, a painful divorce and a brokenhearted husband. How many

marriages are there like this one? There is no way of knowing. I
have counseled two or three such marriages annually.

It has been wisely said that we are as sick as our secrets.
Many homosexually oriented people keep their orientation a
secret. Keeping this secret often entails denying or completely
repressing their sexual feelings because of genuine fear or shame.
We know of many cases in which such shame and lack of acceptance of homosexual feelings have contributed to dysfunctional
lifestyles, compulsive sexual behavior, depression and even suicide. From a pastoral perspective, I believe it is very important
and helpful for homosexual people to acknowledge and accept
the reality of their sexual orientation. Only then can a person
move on to establish the psychological and spiritual tools to live
a sound, chaste life. I believe it is only when sexual feelings are
acknowledged and integrated in one's life that a healthy, chaste
life is truly possible.

A Story of Conversion

My name is Brian. My story is a bit different because I am
not a cradle Catholic. I was baptized as an infant in the
Presbyterian Church. But by the time I reached adulthood, I did
not consider myself a Christian anymore. I had come to believe
that Christianity was responsible for a lot of society's prejudice
against homosexuals. As I reflect on my own history, I was really
angry with God because I thought he made me gay. I rejected
God because I felt God had rejected me. That all began to change
when I met Joe, a devout man who was gay and Catholic.

Joe and I became friends. Eventually we shared a home
together. Joe's commitment to his church baffled me. I thought of
the Catholic Church as a monolithic, centralized power structure

run by Rome and concerned with money, power and control. The paradox was that Joe found the church to be an important source of strength for him.

Eventually Joe was diagnosed with full-blown AIDS. In the course of a year I watched Joe get sicker and sicker. First he got to the point where he could no longer work. Then he had to give up driving. Then he was confined to bed. Then one day he died peacefully in our home. I was alone and filled with grief. I had lost my dearest friend.

My loss created a deep spiritual need. While on a business trip to France, I stopped in a little church run by a community of monks. While visiting the church I had a deep religious experience of God's presence. When I returned to the United States, I wrote a letter to one of the monks I had met at the church. I poured my whole life out to him in the letter and asked the monk what I should do. Was there any hope for me?

I received a letter back with simple advice: "Pray to the Virgin Mary and live in the Eucharist." Every day since Joe's death, I had been saying the rosary. It gave me the feeling of connection with Joe, since the rosary had been part of Joe's wake service. The second piece of advice was more difficult to understand, given my Protestant background. But once I came to believe in the real presence of Jesus in the blessed sacrament, that made all the difference in the world.

I found a wonderful parish where there was an outreach to lesbians and gays. I started attending Mass every Sunday. I started to meet people who were Joe's friends. Before long I just felt part of the community. I entered the RCIA. I never thought that I would last.

We began to share our faith journeys. The leader of the RCIA team gave me a copy of the 1986 *Letter to Bishops of the Catholic Church on the Pastoral Care of Homosexual Persons*. As I read and studied that letter, I had trouble remembering that it was supposed to be all about me as a homosexual person. I did not recognize my life in that letter. Although some of the language was a little harsh, I found it less challenging than some of the gospel calls like: "Sell everything you have and give it to the poor and come, follow me," or "Love your enemies and bless those who curse you." Yet the letter did cause some tensions within me. I decided to go on just the same. I have never regretted my decision to stick it out. I believe that God calls each of us and gives us whatever we need to respond to his call.

✐ A Personal Response

Brian's story calls for some comments. Who could not recognize the providence of God in Brian's long journey in faith? God is always the unseen companion on all of life's journeys, no matter where life leads us. And certainly God does not miss an opportunity to enter in and offer us a call to change our hearts or to offer us a special grace. And sometimes God calls us to walk down paths that are uncharted. Because God accompanies us, he can catch us no matter what path we choose.

I would offer a concern and a caution. Brian should never have been given the *Letter to Bishops of the Catholic Church* to read on his own. First of all, that document, as its very title indicates, is for bishops to read, study and implement as they judge. Such a document was never intended for general consumption. It is a document meant to guide bishops in a proper defense of the church's teaching against certain trends that seemed to question traditional teaching and to provide them with certain principles and guidelines for ministry with homosexual Catholics. How much more pastorally sound and caring it would have been if someone in the RCIA, with proper understanding and training, could have presented the truths and challenges of that pastoral letter with love and sensitivity. Given the complexity of homo-

sexuality and given the difficulties encountered among homosexual people, how could anyone simply hand a person a document
never intended for them?

I Will Return to My Father's House

My name is Martin. When I was in grammar school and
high school, I felt a calling to the priesthood. The nuns were
encouraging to me. Thinking I was the "genuine article," they put
the pressure on me. But as time passed, a different pressure was
building inside of me.

I began to experience confusion over what we now call a sexual orientation. Of course, every time I had an "impure thought,"
I would run off to confession. Yet, no number of Hail Marys or
Our Fathers seemed to help me out of this situation. As more time
went by, it was not just a matter of thoughts that bothered me. It
was all so very confusing. There were no books about homosexuality, as there are today. I could not say anything to my folks. One
priest I spoke to only heightened my fears and confusion with his
own abhorrence of what I described going on inside myself. All I
could hear were the terrible words people used in talking about
someone like me. My greatest pain was going to church and being
confronted with words that marked me for eternal punishment. I
tried so hard and for so long to be good, but failed at being what
everyone else said I was supposed to be.

In college things changed. I was on a secular campus. Being
away from a Catholic atmosphere for the first time in my life
allowed me the freedom to finally confront my demons. I stopped
going to Mass. Soon I left the church. My anger raged at those
whom I judged had cast me out of my faith community. Yet, I

remained very close to God, but now without the structures of my Catholic upbringing.

I felt like I had been orphaned. I had lost my family, the Catholic Church. I would go to Mass on special occasions, but I refrained from receiving communion. My abstinence broke my heart. As I reflect on those days, I believe I was my own worst enemy. I did not see myself as God's beloved child.

About two years ago, a fourteen-year relationship I had with a man came to a crashing halt. I was devastated and lonely. I began to search for the meaning of it all. My life began to turn around. I entered into a journey that I still travel. I began that journey nourished by the constant and unrelenting love of my parents. They had always accepted me. My orientation never created a barrier between myself and them. Another great source of strength for this new turn in my life was provided by two wonderful priests who finally opened doors for me that I thought were barred forever.

It was a Saturday night Mass. I had had a long talk with my pastor the day before which led to an unforgettable moment of sacramental reconciliation. At Mass I sat, stood and knelt with my church. It was suddenly time for communion. I walked down the aisle. Suddenly I found myself looking into the eyes of my pastor. He smiled. Tears were running down my face. I opened my hands. "The body of Christ," he said. I placed the holy bread in my mouth. God was with me. He always was with me. I remain in awe of that moment whenever I am at Mass.

✍ *A Personal Response*

This particular story is especially dear to me. The person who tells this story actually grew up with me. We were members of the same parish. We grew up together. I knew his family. What I did not know or even suspect was his secret. It was only years later that he wrote and told me of his hidden life. What so impresses me is how God manages to be so close to all of us when he seems so far away. This story tells me that God's mercy and love truly are boundless. I have heard so many equally beautiful and powerful stories. How easy it is for us, in our desire and struggle for fidelity, not to recognize God's fidelity to us. We forget because we are too focused on our own efforts and fail to see God's efforts on our behalf. This story is a challenge to our faith. Our openness and vulnerability to God certainly play a part in our salvation. But in the end, it is God's faithfulness that saves us.

My friend Martin discovered God's faithfulness. Martin speaks of two loving parents and two wonderful priests. It is clear that Martin's parents were not nagging, judgmental, anxious or fretful. When we do not fret and are not anxious, we leave a place in our lives for waiting. Waiting is no easy task, but it is an essential ingredient of faith. Waiting is that space and freedom we give to God to accomplish his actions in the lives of people we love. Good parenting knows a lot about waiting.

And what can we say about the two priests? Were they just liberals? Were they rigorists? Rigorists and liberals do not always accomplish what they hope to accomplish. And often enough, they are so strong that they build walls and put up barriers to God's grace. I suspect that the two priests were prudent men. I suspect that they were realists who recognized sin where there was sin and could name grace where there was grace. I strongly suspect they were in touch with their own frailty and brokenness. I have no doubt that somehow they entered into some of Martin's pain. It seems that God is able to use our vulnerability and our humility as channels for his grace.

I Won't Be Coming Back

How wonderful it was to hear you speak at St. Stephen's Episcopal last night. I am the one who brought his Catholic parents to hear you. My partner and I helped establish DIGNITY before it was banned by the archbishop. We were saddened and hurt by that unfortunate event. DIGNITY was helpful to my parents when I first came out.

I have had a love-hate relationship with the Catholic Church. I value the spirituality you brought to us last night in your talk. It is what I miss so much. Your own love for the Catholic Church astounds me. As a man living with AIDS, I have come to find myself loved and nurtured at St. Stephen's. Yet, I do miss "something" you spoke about, which is nonintellectual but, rather, felt by the heart, something only Catholics can know and experience about Catholicism. I experience a void at times when I am among non-Catholics. I still identify with being Catholic, but if I were to die tomorrow, I would want to be buried from St. Stephen's. But you do inspire me to stay in touch and not to stray too far away. Thank you, Father.

A Personal Response

How difficult it is to comment on the mystery of presence and distance from the church in one man's life. I do recall Jesus speaking of having other sheep not of his fold. I recall strong images of Jesus used to describe discipleship: a light on a lamp stand, the light of the world and the salt of the earth. Sometimes we are a link in the bond with those alienated from our church when we least expect it. The night I went to St. Stephen's to speak, I did not think my words or my commitment to the church were going to mean anything special to anyone there, but they did. I suppose it is only logical that a happy ending to this story would be that a year from now, our friend would return to the Catholic Church. I would certainly want that. If he does not return, my labors were not in vain. Our success is sometimes not always marked by a positive outcome. Our success lies in our always being heralds of the gospel.

This chapter gave some people an opportunity to tell their story. You had an opportunity to listen. Listening is a powerful tool in ministry. And it is especially essential in effective ministry with homosexual persons. They do not get to tell their stories very often. People presume they already know their stories. And there are some who simply do not want to hear their stories. How often I have heard homosexual persons say to me: "Oh, my parents know I am gay, but they just never want to talk about it." How can we presume to know anyone unless we listen to them? How can we know anyone without knowing some of his or her story? And

what message are we sending if we think we either already know what the story is or do not want to hear it in the first place? It is in our personal stories that we find the grace and presence of God working in our lives. Homosexual Catholics are talked about, written about and are objects of concern or neglect. But only recently have there been some meager efforts to listen to their stories.

Listening is not easy. If I begin to listen, my own agenda can stop up my ears. My feelings of discomfort, my morbid curiosity, my personal judgments and

"Whoever receives you receives me."
Matthew 10:40

my fears can turn my heart to stone. To be willing to put my agenda aside is to make a sacrifice. Such a sacrifice is a kind of self-emptying through which the person speaking receives my undivided attention. Listening is an attitude that involves more than my sense of hearing. Listening involves one's heart. Jesus is a model for listening to our homosexual sisters and brothers.

Chapter 7

Where Do You Stand?

What is the state of the question? It goes without saying that homosexuality is a question of great complexity and controversy. Father Richard Sparks, C.S.P., has written and lectured extensively on the topic. At a recent religious education congress sponsored by the Archdiocese of Los Angeles at the Anaheim Convention Center in California, Father Sparks suggested a spectrum of positions that various people take regarding homosexuality. I find Father Sparks's observations very helpful. I offer his positions here for your own reflection and understanding. My intention is neither to fuel controversy nor to end it, nor do I wish to advocate for this or that position. My intention is to define and explain the various positions so that you may understand the differing outlooks and opinions people have as we continue to debate and discuss homosexuality. Such information may help you understand a friend, relative or an adult child who is homosexual. The spectrum that Father Sparks presents goes from a *far right position* to a *far left position*. In between the two extremes are positions of full acceptance, qualified acceptance and the traditional Catholic position. I want to say something about each position.

Those who take a far right position might simply state that homosexuality is sinful. In describing homosexuality as sinful, no distinction is made between the inclination and the sexual acting out of the inclination; both are sinful. Homosexuality, in any of its dimensions, is simply a perversion. Persons who labor with homosexual feelings and attractions are to be pitied. Authentic

ministry to such persons is all about convincing them to leave the
homosexual lifestyle and to return to their natural heterosexual
state.

Who would hold the far right position? Many biblical fun-
damentalists would certainly share such a view, as well as many
who could be described as ultraconservative in their mentality.
Also sharing such a view would be certain charismatic prayer
groups who are heavily influenced by a fundamentalistic
approach to the scripture and, in general, totally ignorant of the
church's teaching on homosexuality. Also within the same camp
would be those who actually inflict grave bodily and psychological harm on homosexual persons or those who might appear to be
homosexual.

Those from the far left position would hold an all-embrac-
ing liberality: "If it feels good, do it." All or any sexual genital
activity is good and natural. It is no one's business what people do
in the privacy of their own lives. No one should be restrained in
the area of sexual pleasure. People should be free to enjoy sex with
whomever they choose. Who would be proponents of such a
position? Radical gay/lesbian rights groups would hold such a
view.

The traditional Catholic/Christian position holds that
being homosexual is not sinful. It is acting on such impulses that
would always and everywhere be sinful. In a perfectly ordered
world, everyone would be heterosexual. But some people are
homosexual, and if they are, their orientation would be an "objective disorder." However, since one's homosexual orientation is
discovered, not chosen, it can never be morally wrong to be
homosexual (gay or lesbian). However, one is not supposed to
perform homosexual genital actions, since these acts are against
the heterosexual norm or order of nature. How then are homosexual persons to live within the Christian community? They, like
all Christians, are required to live chaste lives. A chaste life in

such circumstances would automatically be a call to live celibately, like all single and unmarried persons.

Who holds such a position? It must be assumed that all practicing Catholics hold this position because it is the official position of the church. In practice, there are exceptions. Anyone who holds a position of authority is expected to believe and support this position. All bishops, by reason of their teaching position in the church, hold to this position. Very often, the historical mainline Protestant churches uphold the Catholic position.

Some people follow what can be called a *qualified acceptance position*. Such persons would agree in principle that in an ideal and perfect world, all persons ought to be heterosexual. However, the reality is that a significant number of men and women are homosexual in orientation. If homosexual persons are called to live a chaste life, then they should not engage in homosexual genital activity. If, however, a homosexual person feels called to live in a monogamous lesbian or gay union, genital expressions should be considered morally acceptable, by way of exception.

Who holds this qualified acceptance position? Not a few homosexual Catholics hold this position. Certain Catholic theologians such as Father Charles Curran would teach such a position. Theologians who have publicly taken such a position can no longer teach in Catholic institutions.

Some hold a *full acceptance position*. People who hold for full acceptance would probably agree that there is really no such thing as a heterosexual norm. Every individual person must discern his or her own dominant orientation. Once a homosexual orientation is determined, the next decision is to remain single or enter into an intimate commitment or union with another person of the same sex. If sexual activity is one of the expressions of commitment, the morality of such actions is governed by the degree of love and commitment between the two persons, rather than some objective and unchangeable moral good that knows no exception.

Who would hold such a view? John McNeil, a gay Catholic and former member of the Society of Jesus, an outspoken writer and critic of traditional church teaching on the subject, would be one. A number of gay and lesbian Catholics would also hold this position.

Yes, all these positions, some of which are totally contrary to church teaching, are held by various practicing and nonpracticing Catholic people. We need not be surprised that there is such disagreement in spite of clear and consistent church teaching on the issue of homosexuality. One can also find such disagreement with the teachings on birth control, in vitro fertilization, abortion, divorce, euthanasia and any number of other teachings. Such positions are sometimes based on conscious and willful dissent or may simply stem from ignorance. Whatever the case, controversy is no stranger in the church.

Guidelines in Controversy

Some controversy is normal and healthy in our church. Controversy is as old as the church itself. Do these questions from the scripture not tell us as much? Mary, on the occasion of the angel's annunciation, asks: "How shall this be since I do not know man?" And recall these questions put to his disciples. "Who do you say that I am?" And the response is noteworthy: "Some say you are John the Baptizer, others Elijah, still others, one of the prophets." "And you," he said, "who do you say that I am?" And remember all the argumentation among the apostles about who was the greatest? And Jesus' question: "What were you discussing on the way?" And when Jesus warned about the dangers of wealth to salvation, the apostles' shocking response: "Who then can be saved?" And think of Jesus' most merciful actions of forgiveness and the response of some: "On what authority do you do such things?"

The scriptures are full of such questions from saints and sinners, because people of faith always yearn to know more and more about the truth. Even the most solemnly defined teaching does not exhaust the mysteries of faith. For example, there is so much more we can know about the Eucharist or the most blessed Trinity.

However, there are guidelines and limitations in our searching and in our questions. Whenever there is controversy in the church, there will be a response or reaction from both its conservative as well as its liberal wings. The church's health and holiness depend on the interaction between these two elements, which can be called the two sides of the truth. There is a necessary and healthy tension between conservative Catholics and liberal Catholics. In and through that tension, we deepen our belief and understanding of the mysteries of faith. Many have pointed out that one of the major problems of our day in the church is that instead of a healthy tension between conservatives and liberals, we now have substituted hostility. Liberals and conservatives no longer speak with one another, they simply condemn the "opposing" side. We need to mend the rift between liberals and conservatives.

Maybe we need to define our terms here. Who is a real conservative? A real conservative is one whose energy and focus is given to protecting and defending what has always been believed and taught by the church. Without a healthy bit of conservatism on the part of every Catholic, our church would be nothing more than a debating society rather than a community of faith. If you are a conservative, you are a gift to the church.

Who is a real liberal? A real liberal is one whose energy and focus is given to developing a deeper understanding of the mysteries of faith. True liberals aid in the development of doctrine. Without healthy liberals, the church would end up being a

static community marked by a rigid and sterile relationship with
God and an inability to grow in wisdom and knowledge. For all
of its orthodoxy, such a faith community would be lacking in
spontaneity and freedom.

What is the marvel of the true conservative and liberal is
their balance and loyalty. They both know what the issue is in
the church at a particular moment. And while each of them may
certainly have a particular agenda, they do not confuse their
agenda with the issue. And there is one more marvel. Both the
true conservative and the true liberal are unquestionably
grounded in what I call the *radical center*. The radical center is
none other than the two sources of our Catholic faith: sacred
scripture and tradition. I call scripture and tradition the radical
center because scripture and tradition are not ends in themselves. You and I are not faithful Catholics because we can quote
the right chapter and verse and its meaning or because we are in
sync with tradition. No, we are loyal and faithful Catholics
because the very foundation of scripture and tradition is the
risen Lord Jesus Christ, who alone is the Lord and Teacher of
the church. Whatever the question raised in the church, no matter how crucial, no matter the consequences, we can only go so
far left or right of center. And that is what happens in any controversy in the church. We always find our way through the crisis brought on by the controversy. When all is said and done, we
find our way back to the radical center, either with some development of doctrine or a decision that the issue is clearly not in
harmony with scripture and tradition.

Oh, if it were only that simple! If the church could always
be so healthy. But it is not. In a time of controversy there are
always some who go too far to the left or too far to the right.
Thus, we speak of the far right and the far left. Such folks are neither truly liberal nor conservative, though they like the titles!

In the heat of controversy, they totally lose sight of the *issue*.

Actually, they have substituted their agenda for the issue. What do these folks have in common? The far right and the far left share anger, fear and a total lack of a sense of humor. If the church does not recognize and embrace their agenda, the church will surely fall apart. Those on the far left like to say that they are prophetic, a title usually recognized and conferred by others and only long after the fact. People on the far right like to call themselves orthodox. Far left and far right simply go too far from the radical center. For all their orthodoxy and prophecy, I have long suspected that within these extreme positions, the groundwork is laid for either heresy or schism in the history of the church.

How does all of this apply to the burning issue of homosexuality? Well, I would invite you to look back to Father Sparks's various positions on homosexuality. You can decide whether any of these positions is conservative or liberal or too far left or right. An example of a far left position would be: "Unless marriage as a sacrament is conferred on all gay and lesbian Catholics, no one can speak of the church being welcoming and hospitable to homosexual Catholics." A far right position might read like this: "Homosexuality is wrong and sinful. The only good homosexual is a changed and cured homosexual. The only place in the church for the homosexual is the psychiatrist's couch or the confessional."

I wrote this chapter with the alienated gay and lesbian Catholic very much in mind. If you meet a gay or lesbian individual who has assumed one of the positions mentioned above, you may now have a better understanding as to where that person is coming from.

I want to close with two letters: one from a gay son to his mother, and the other from a mother to her gay son. In our various responses to homosexuality, where on the spectrum would you find these two persons?

Dear Mom:

This letter is the result of a new development in the area of my individuality. I want to be separate, yet closer to you, Dad and the rest of the family. In the past year, I have discovered and accepted much more of who I am and always have been. I have wanted to tell you many times in the past year but certain planned occasions (such as Yosemite) have fallen through when the entire family was together. And, it seems there is no perfect time.

I want to be closer, and I want to be more open about my personal life. I have never wanted anything else. I am also sick of hiding who I am. It's not fair to me or anyone else. If you have not guessed it, I am now ready to tell you that I am gay. I have always been. I am also gay-happy. I am telling you this out of love, I don't have AIDS.

I have known for at least ten years but have only fully accepted it within the last year. It has made me much happier too. I have always been this way, and I am sure of who I am. I denied and rejected my identity because of the fear of rejection due to old-world Catholic teachings and a largely uninformed society that, in general, does not encourage or acknowledge the validity of any deviation from what may be considered "average" or "normal." I no longer believe what I am told to believe. I decide for myself. Negative judgments even caused me to pray for "healing." I am sure that the healing I needed is what I have now. I have a greater feeling of self-worth, self-esteem and love of myself.

I have come to believe that I am part of the diversity of God's creation. God chose to make me the way I am. God does not make mistakes. I am telling you first because I am closest to you. I do not want to hurt your feelings by telling another member of the family first. I have told some people in the choir for their support and advice. It was easier to tell them. I do not care who knows. Everyone can use her or his own discretion in telling others. I am prepared for possible rejection and realize that I cannot deal with other people's problems for them. I know that my family and true friends will still love me. Their love is what is important to me. I can handle whatever happens. I know the Lord is on my side.

Do not worry. God has taken pretty damn good care of me throughout my life and is not going to stop caring now. Why do you think Father Michele had you read the book *Are You Still My Mother?* The latter was not my doing. I may disagree with the church on a few things. Yet, the church is part of me. I am part of the church. The church is my home. The Lord is my best friend. He has always been there for me. This is mainly why I turned out okay.

I want to tell you that there is no love interest in my life right now and there has never been one in the past. I can be happy living the rest of my life single and celibate, but such a life would not leave me the happiest I could be. I dream of finding another person to love deeply. I would want the same love from him. I have so much love inside that has been held back for so long. I want a lifetime relationship. I want commitment. I do not want a promiscuous lifestyle.

You and Dad have taught me the value of love, truth, honesty, kindness, caring and patience. The Lord gave me the both of you as parents so as to prepare me well for life. God chose well. I know how blessed I am. I know that no one has any reason to fear or to hate me for being different. I find peace and comfort in such knowledge.

There are many other people out there experiencing what I already have experienced. They live with incredible fear. So many folks are still hiding as I once did. I hope my own "coming out" will also help them. There is too much hate and fear out there.

Love you Mom and Dad,

Tim

Dear Tim,

When you first told me you had something to tell me, I asked if you were getting married. You answered: "No!" I then imagined the worst. Maybe you lost your job, your apartment. Maybe something awful happened. The next morning at breakfast, on my birthday, you told me you were gay. My response was "Is that all?" I was relieved. Now I realize how perfect my response was at the time. Yet my emotions were saying something else. I had a lot to sift through. You helped me get through that initial news. You even gave me flowers and asked if I noticed that one was different, like my children.

Your revelation was now my coming out. I was on a journey. I had to find out all I could. So many tears began to fall from my eyes after I hugged you and got into the car. I cried constantly for three weeks. Your dad was concerned. He asked me why I was doing this to myself; I could not help it.

I was in grief. I was grieving over what I thought your life was supposed to be. I did not think it was possible anymore for you to be happy. I saw couples walking down the street and holding hands. I thought you would never be able to experience that kind of love and companionship. I would see children. Children just naturally flock to you. You would have been such a great dad. And I would cry some more. The following evening, the news still fresh, you seemed like a different person. You were not the person I imagined you were. I cried again.

I shared your letter with a priest friend. He said he never doubted that you were truly gay. I made fruitless efforts to find information in two bookstores. I found nothing. When I was still crying a week later, Father gave me the name and the number of another mother in P-FLAG (Parents and Family and Friends of Lesbians and Gays). She talked with me at length. She sent me information and the phone number of another Catholic parent. She told me something that made all the difference in the world. She assured me that I did not make you gay.

How I wished our church had prepared me for your special coming into this world. Just knowing the possibility that I could have had a gay child would have made things easier. You have shared that you knew about yourself for a long time and that you only lately had been able to accept yourself. I thank God all the time that you were not one of the suicide statistics. Instead, you are an incredible gift to our family. I love you!

With Much Love,

Mom

A Final Word

Homosexuality is never going to go away. The controversy in society will most probably be resolved long before it is resolved within the Catholic Church. The church moves slowly because it seeks the will of God. The will of God is not always what is popular or obvious. And how homosexuality and all its ramifications will be resolved in society will no doubt be at odds with the teaching of the church. The church by its very nature and call is less than at home with everything that is taken for granted in the secular world. There is no way out of this dilemma because Jesus was always countercultural. He took little for granted and, with the eyes of faith, tried to fathom in the depths of life the hand and the will of his Father. Therefore it was not uncommon for him to be at odds with the world around him. Be that as it may, I am also confident that the church has much to learn about homosexuality and the plight of those who discover this as an unchanging reality in their lives. This book is intended to help us enter into a process of deeper discernment, because the last word has not been spoken about homosexuality.

There are forces within society and church who want nothing more than to rid both society and the church of any trace of homosexuality. Many such persons may be sincere and upright people of faith. But some have evil desires and will stoop to any means to get their way. They will lie, distort information and stir up controversy that lays the foundation for violence and hostility toward homosexual men and women and children. Such persons are intent on doing great harm. How shall we respond? We are powerless to stop them. But our witness against their ways is answer enough.

Our attitude is important. Homosexuality can be viewed as a problem to be solved. We can also view homosexuality as one of the mysteries of life. We live with mysteries. We allow mysteries to invite us to deal with realities in such a way that our resolution and decisions lead us to a primacy of respect and reverence for persons. Homosexuality always exists in persons like Tim, who are sexual human beings. Persons of homosexual orientation have legitimate needs to love and to care. They need to escape from isolation and enter into community. Homosexuality is about persons on a journey. We all journey together. If we dare to walk together, we will meet difference and paradox in those we walk with. Walking together does not always mean finding easy solutions to our differences. Rather, we will find responses coming from deep within the recesses of our hearts that clearly echo the gospel of Jesus Christ. That journey will be long and arduous, not without risk or the tears of a mother for her homosexual child. Our homosexual Catholics and their parents have walked too long alone. No one need walk alone.

Chapter 8

"Always Our Children"

"Educationally, homosexuality cannot and ought not to be skirted or ignored. The topic 'must be faced in all objectivity by the pupil and the educator when the case presents itself.'"[1] These words may sound like the sentiments of a gay activist. The truth is that these are the words of our American bishops, who recommend that homosexuality has to be talked about in schools because there may be students present who are trying to accept their own homosexual orientation. For some people, the very notion of homosexual youth is shocking. We take for granted that all homosexual people are adults. But think again. It is true that full and certain awareness of a homosexual identity is often only articulated after childhood and the teen years, when one is more fully an adult. But it would hardly be correct to think that a homosexual adult suddenly emerges on one's twenty-first birthday.

There is a considerable amount of data confirming that the foundations for adult homosexuality are laid in early childhood and adolescence. Such data reveals: (1) that homosexual activity among adolescents is not all that rare or unusual; it does happen. (2) Same-sex genital activity by itself is not an absolute guarantee that an adolescent is truly homosexual or that such experimentation will lead that youth into becoming homosexual. (3) There are a growing number of adolescents who now declare themselves as homosexually oriented. (4) Many homosexual adolescents and adult homosexual persons speak of childhood memories and behavior that signaled to them that they were always different from their peers. When they felt ready, they named that reality and shared it with whomever they felt safe to do so. Such disclosures cannot simply be dismissed because they may cause discomfort or raise disconcerting questions. We are obligated to receive such secrets as serious self-disclosures motivated by courage and honesty and a desire to preserve one's integrity.

When such confidences are shared with us, we had best pause for a moment of reflection and prayer before we dare respond. It is good to realize that we can respond to the news in any number of ways, depending on how we feel about homosexuality. We need to be aware that our primary response is to a person, not to the information shared with us. We need to stretch beyond our understandable fears and questions and realize that what has been confided to us is something that comes out of the core of a person's life and gives shape to every waking moment. It would be helpful to let the person know that you are open to hearing that story without prying or meddling.

The American bishops have accepted the reality of an early development of homosexual orientation and it is they who are the authors of the opening words of this chapter. They go on to add:

> First and foremost, we support modeling and teaching respect for every human person, regardless of sexual orientation. Second, a parent or teacher must also present clearly and delicately the unambiguous moral norms of the Christian tradition regarding homosexual genital activity, appropriately geared to the age level and maturity of the learner. Finally, parents and other educators must remain open to the possibility that a particular person, whether adolescent or adult, may be struggling to accept his or her own orientation. The distinction between being homosexual and doing homosexual genital actions, while not always clear and convincing, is a helpful and important one when deal-

ing with the complex issue of homosexuality, particularly in the educational and pastoral arena.[2]

It is important to understand what the bishops are saying and what they are not saying. They are not suggesting or encouraging educators and parents to accept a flamboyant style of life so often portrayed in the media, a style that invites ridicule and rejection. The bishops are not suggesting that adolescents take to the streets and march in a gay pride parade or join the gay rights movement. The bishops are not advocating the acceptance of a style of life that is contrary to traditional Catholic doctrine about sex and morals. The bishops are not giving license for same-sex genital activity. In fact, the bishops do make a distinction between the inclination toward homosexual activity and acting upon such an inclination.

Unfortunately and inaccurately, many people believe that having a homosexual orientation is synonymous with being sexually active. Such an attitude, while understandable, is seriously flawed. Such a belief makes it difficult for anyone to talk about a same-sex orientation. Such an attitude contributes to an environment of secrecy and suspicion and leads to false judgments and stereotyping of all homosexually oriented persons. It is such a mentality that contributes to an unnecessary enmity and division between homosexual adolescents and their parents. Fostering such a mentality destroys and undermines family unity where one member of the family is homosexual.

The bishops are most certainly not advocating what many loosely refer to as *the gay lifestyle*. The bishops are not suggesting that an adolescent announce and proclaim his or her orientation for the entire world to hear. Indiscriminate coming out could be naive and premature. A youth just awakening to homosexual feelings could be very confused and overwhelmed. He or she has hardly had the time to recognize and integrate sexual feelings into their lives. More likely than not, a youth may not be able to handle the hostility and judgments of his or her peers at a time when conforming and a sense of belonging are important to a teenager. There is also the risk of prejudice on the part of uninformed teachers, counselors and parents or even one's pastor.

I recently received a phone call from a self-declared sixteen-year-old boy who came out to his confirmation class. The pastor removed the youth from the confirmation program and asked the boy to leave his parish because parents might fear the influence and example of an openly homosexual youth. That decision was based on both unfounded fear and ignorance of church teaching and sound pastoral practice.

Cultural attitudes and values toward homosexuality also have to be considered. One's culture is a strong influence and clearly frames our opinions and attitudes toward the world and social interaction and homosexuality. If one's culture is also Catholic, the values of the culture are often identified with Catholic teaching. Are you more American than Catholic? If you are Hispanic, do your cultural attitudes square with official Catholic teaching? If you are African American, do your cultural attitudes agree with the official teaching of the Catholic Church? If you are one of the Asian Pacific peoples, do your cultural attitudes support and confirm Catholic teaching on homosexuality? In most ethnic concerns around homosexuality, cultural attitudes and values are often at odds with official Catholic teaching and pastoral approaches. It is therefore paramount to understand what the official teaching is saying. It is equally important to adjust and adapt cultural attitudes toward homosexuality so that they conform to church teaching and pastoral concerns. Unfortunately, it is just the opposite that often happens. Culture tends to shape or obscure Catholic teaching. I once heard a prominent leader of Asian Pacific ministries explain that Asian cultures are very supportive of the church's teachings on homosexuality. She explained that homosexuality was, in fact, nonexistent in Asian cultures and became problematic only when Asian peoples came to live in the United States and were introduced to homosexuality.

What the bishops are saying is that awareness of homosexual orientation is real and can be frightening to the adolescent who is awakening to such feelings and inclinations. The bishops are also deeply aware of and sensitive to the fact that such feelings may be understandably disturbing to parents who receive the news that their son or daughter is homosexual.

It is quite common and understandable that a homosexual teenager would tend to keep his or her feelings a deep and dark secret. The homosexual adolescent may feel seriously flawed by the simple fact of such feelings and tendencies. Did God make some terrible mistake? It is not untypical for a homosexual youth to pray to God for deliverance from such feelings. When deliverance does not come, he or she may feel abandoned by God or simply accursed. If one feels rejected by God, it follows that the church might be equally rejecting and unwelcoming. I meet too many homosexual Catholics who have not only left the church but who feel a tremendous anger toward the church for these very reasons.

Who has not witnessed news reports of gay pride parades and celebrations? In the reporting of such events, you will inevitably see gay activists dressed as nuns and priests, sporting religious habits, sacred vestments, miters, pectoral crosses and crosiers. Understandably, the media is attracted to such displays of sensationalism. Such irreverence and disrespect is distasteful and offensive to Catholic sensibilities. Among far-right Catholics, such outrageous behavior is oftentimes met with equally outrageous statements that accomplish nothing and actually fuel the fires of hatred against our Catholic Church. When rage meets rage, the perceived enemy has achieved its goal, which I have come to believe is negative attention.

What is little appreciated is that many of those who wage such a war of irreverence and disrespect against our church are themselves alienated Roman Catholics. I recall a Mass offered for persons living with AIDS. Cardinal Mahony, archbishop of Los Angeles was presiding and anointing the sick who were suffering with full-blown AIDS. The church was filled with AIDS patients. Outside, one could hear the shouts of those protesting the Mass. When Mass was ended, I recall processing out of the church. All along the street were members of Act-Up, a gay rights activist group. These people were jeering and taunting at everyone, including the cardinal. The cardinal, totally unruffled by such antics, invited some of those folks into the reception that followed the Mass! Many of those protesting were ex-Catholics. The leader was the nephew of the bishop of a large midwestern diocese. In speaking with them that night, I learned that their major grievance was that they believed our church had failed to speak out about AIDS and about serious prejudice and violence against gay people! I remembered the signs they carried that night around the church: "Silence = Death." I felt vulnerable to the moment. I tried to get in touch with that silence, to listen to its sounds. Was there a message here?

They told tales of silence. They spoke of a silence that never prays for homosexual people or their parents in our solemn Sunday gatherings when we pray for almost everyone and everything. They spoke of a silence that fails to present church teaching in a clear and sensitive way. They told of a silence that fails to give support to an archdiocesan program for homosexual persons and their parents. They told of a silence where official family life ministry simply fails to address the issue of homosexuality. They told of a silence that never decried the violent murder of Matthew Shepard.

These sounds of silence are not missed by homosexual Catholics. And more and more, those sounds of silence make a din for the ears of their loving parents, who are beginning to speak out on behalf of their baptized homosexual sons and daughters. The sounds of silence are louder and more dangerous than outright prejudice and condemnation. Silence carries a clear and painful message: "You do not matter." As one aging lesbian couple, pillars of their parish, confided to me one day after Mass: "Father, they do not know we are here. If we left tomorrow, no one would notice or feel our absence." What an indictment.

The lessons of silence are learned early in the lives of homosexual youths struggling with their homosexuality. Gay jokes and words like *fag* and *dyke* at school may set in motion attitudes of shame and feelings of being evil or sick. Research shows that homosexual adolescents suffer a great deal of psychological and emotional turmoil over issues associated with the acceptance or nonacceptance of their homosexual orientation. Such turmoil is often hidden in the self-imposed silence and isolation of a homosexual youth.

What does the homosexual youth do in his or her silence and isolation? He or she typically internalizes the negative messages they hear. That boy who was dismissed from his confirmation class and asked to leave his parish could easily feel that there is something essentially wrong with him beyond God's mercy and the concern of the church. Such a youth may easily consider suicide, especially if there is reason to believe that his parents may disown or reject him. Other more typical behaviors may follow, such as sexual promiscuity, prostitution, drugs and other risky behaviors. And sometimes it happens that a youth becomes so confused and lacking in direction that he or she might think that there are no choices but to live out the stereotype of a homosexual as painted and depicted by prejudice, fear and ignorance.

If families, parishes, Catholic schools, religious education programs, youth programs and young adult programs remain unconscious and unwelcoming of the presence of homosexual persons, then we have failed to minister to a segment of our Catholic people. Such persons remain unknown to us because, in our unconsciousness of them, we relegate them to silence and isolation, forcing them to deal alone with issues that already separate them from the mainstream and mainstays of a healthy community. The church should not be surprised when such persons seek and find acceptance and community in a gay subculture. Such gay subculture communities are accessible in most large cities. It is inaccurate to condemn or depict these communities as places of corruption whose sole intent is to ensnare the innocent into the gay lifestyle. To be sure, such ghettos have a destructive dimension. Nonetheless, places of this kind may also offer a sense of community and wholesome entertainment and recreation in a comparatively safe environment.

Yet if Catholic homosexual persons are going to be able to make healthy choices about what is offered within the gay subculture, then they have to have an assurance that the church is their primary community where, as openly homosexual people, they are truly nourished and nurtured on many levels.

It happens now more and more that a healthy homosexual youth who is dealing with an evolving understanding of his or her own homosexuality will seek out a teacher, a counselor, a priest, a religious or layperson with whom to confide his or her secret. How might you respond if you were chosen for such a task?

Take your first clue from gospel hospitality. Create a safe environment for such a youth. Assure him or her of your profound respect for courageously dealing with such a frightening reality. Ask respectful questions such as: *How can I be of help? How did you come to realize this about yourself? Was it scary for you? When did you first realize this about yourself? Has it been difficult? Have you shared with anyone else? How did they respond? What is your greatest fear?* It is helpful to remind them that you hope that they never forget that God loves them—not because of or in spite of their orientation but simply because God loves us all as we are.

It is wise to suggest that such a student do some reading on the subject. It is inadvisable to recommend reading official church documents on homosexuality unless you first offer some background on understanding such documents. Such documents are resources for priests, teachers and counselors; they are technical documents and can be very confusing and misleading if they are read without assistance. If you do judge that a particular document might be helpful, know that you had better supply pastoral sensitivity and understanding as a background for understanding church teaching. What is important is that church teaching on this subject be presented with the utmost care and sensitivity because the church is not in a position to offer any hope of sexual fulfillment or a union that would be comparable to the commitment we find in the sacrament of matrimony. I do not find it helpful to hide or compromise the teaching of the church. Somewhere on his or her travels, the homosexual Catholic will encounter the truth and will then have to deal with church teaching. Do not patronize or overprotect a homosexual youth. Your love and acceptance will go a long way in helping him or her deal with whatever paradox or pain church teaching may cause.

Because of a lack of experience, a homosexual youth may think that your own positive attitude toward him or her is shared by everyone else. Gently remind the young person that this simply is not so. Although church people usually have a predisposition to love unconditionally in imitation of God's unconditional love for us, not all achieve this perfectly. Safety for the homosexual youth is paramount. Remind such a person not to be naive about prejudice and even possible violence from members of the church and society. Make sure that the young person knows that they have their entire lives to adjust to his or her sexual orientation. One need not rush to understand fully. Finally, while it is very important to come out to someone, coming out more generally is something to do slowly and with real thought. It could be premature to come out to everyone before one is fully clear about what it means for him or her to be homosexual.

In *Is It a Choice?* Eric Marcus writes:

> The statistics on suicide sadly confirm how unhappy
> many people are about being gay or lesbian—espe-
> cially while they're first dealing with their feelings of
> attraction for the same sex....Some studies say that 40
> percent of all homosexuals make attempts on their
> lives when they're young....And one-third of teenage
> suicides involve gay and lesbian teens.[3]

In the *Report of the Secretary's Task Force on Youth Suicide,*
released by the Department of Health and Human Services
(DHHS) in 1989, the government reported that gay and lesbian
youth are two to three times more likely to commit suicide than
heterosexual youth.

Ideally, every homosexual person should be able to tell his
or her parents about their homosexuality. And every parent also
has the right to know and understand such a reality in the life of
his or her child. But such sharing is not always possible or advisable. Very often, an adolescent will have a good sense of when or
whether it is advisable to share such information with his or her
parents. What is most important is to advise such a youth to continue to share with you and not to isolate him- or herself regarding ongoing questions and concerns about homosexuality.

It is unfortunate but well substantiated that most of the
homosexual youth out on the streets or prostituting themselves
are young persons who have been condemned by their parents or
ousted from their homes. Education of parents must be given first
order of priority.

It is important for a teacher, priest or counselor to have a
sense of his or her own comfort or discomfort when dealing with
the subject of homosexuality. Positive and negative feelings are
easily picked up by homosexual persons who early on in their

lives developed a keen awareness of present hostility as a means of survival in a hostile world.

If a youth is romantically involved with another homosexual youth, what action can or should be taken? When it comes to sexual relations or experimentation, what is said and expected of heterosexual young people is equally applicable to a homosexual youth. It must be remembered that the church respects and supports a stable platonic friendship between two homosexual persons. It forbids only what may be called a "gay marriage" that assumes to take on as legitimate and life-giving what is limited to traditional marriage.

It will be most helpful here to point out that no one, no matter what their orientation or state in life, is expected to live without genuine signs of affection and physical touch. No one is forbidden to enter deep and lasting relationships. Some signs of (nongenital) affection are appropriate for all, given the proper circumstance. North American culture tends to be restrained in affection, especially affection shared by men with one another. I want to say that our American practices are neither necessarily virtuous nor universally accepted. Our social customs certainly are safe but not very healthy. We send mixed messages to our homosexual sisters and brothers. For example, a heterosexual vowed religious and priest are allowed a spontaneity once forbidden them. Priests and nuns today enjoy particular friends, they dance at weddings, are hugged, touched and kissed. No one is scandalized at such displays of affection that seem so normal and human. We need to avoid setting up standards for homosexual persons that exceed standards required of the rest of the Catholic community.

I recognize that the thoughts expressed in these pages are challenging to most of us. It is regrettable that we have more questions than answers when we deal with homosexuality. We need to examine our attitudes. If we had not been so distant from the plight of our homosexual relatives and friends and their families, we would have a whole collection of wisdom to help us. We had best not waste time and energy berating ourselves and lamenting our past. We need to forgive ourselves for the negligence and blindness of the past and boldly move to sincere care and concern. Our sincerity will be tested. We are bound to make mistakes along the way to inclusiveness and regard. We have every reason to be hopeful about our efforts because we do have a context and basis for our response to homosexual persons. That context is our constant teaching and belief that every human person, no matter what the circumstances, has an inherent worth and dignity that must always be respected. Respect for human dignity is the foundation for our outreach to homosexual persons.

If our proper response to homosexuality is rooted in a respect for human dignity, it finds another basic context in the family. Every homosexual person is born of a mother and a father. Taking homosexuality out of the context of family life is a serious mistake that has dire consequences. Recently the bishops of the United States wrote a pastoral letter to the parents of homosexual children. The name of that letter, *Always Our Children*,[4] has become a household phrase in ministry with homosexual Catholics these days. I would like to conclude this chapter by recommending and commenting on the content and implications of this pastoral message.

I know of no other official document that has ever addressed the parents of homosexual children in the way this document does. Clearly new ground has been broken here. I mean to say that a long silence has been broken. Given the fact that parents are the primary educators of their children, how did we fail to consider their role in the life of a homosexual son or daughter? How did we not recognize that such a son or daughter would have siblings who would be deeply affected by the homosexual orientation of their brother or sister? Perhaps we were so distanced from homosexual persons that we never thought of them as related to parents and family. We never considered the feelings present in these families.

For the longest time, when treating homosexuality, our only concern and preoccupation was with sin and keeping homosexual persons out of the occasions of sin. Now, we are looking at homosexuality from a more complete perspective. Homosexual persons are always our children. Is this not a shift in our thinking? Is this not a healthier attitude? One can only imagine where all of this will lead the church. Will the church not be more careful and sensitive in its pronouncements? Will it not be more responsive to parents who passionately plead for and defend their children? How can such parents remain indifferent to the fact that the vast majority of their children find themselves outside of the church or alienated from the faith because an orientation the church claims is not chosen. No, the mood is clearly changing. Listen to these opening words of *Always Our Children*.

> This message is not intended for advocacy purposes or to serve a particular agenda. It is not to be understood as an endorsement of what some call "a homosexual lifestyle."
>
> *Always Our Children* is an outstretched hand of the bishops' Committee on Marriage and Family to parents and other family members, offering them a fresh look at the grace present in family life and the unfailing mercy of Christ our Lord.[5]

The document wisely asks parents to be in touch, not with their children first, but with their own feelings, no matter what those feelings may be. If parents do not sift through their feelings, name and own them, those feelings will become so many obstacles in the way of building their relationship with their children. A list of feelings is offered. Many parents feel relief because they always suspected their child was homosexual. Others will feel anger or the need to blame. Still others may have to grieve real losses and hopes now changed forever. Some parents feel fear. Is my son in sin? Can my daughter receive communion? Will people hate my child or harm him? Still other parents may feel guilt, shame or loneliness. Did I make my child this way? What will people say or think?

Once they know and name their feelings, parents are then urged to make a conscious effort to love and accept their children. They learn to give proper consideration to their children's orientation and its influence in shaping life and faith. The bishops offer a number of suggestions, which are not so much answers as they are guiding principles of faith and pastoral concern. I summarize the following principles briefly, hoping to entice parents and educators to read and study the bishops' document in its entirety.

1. Accept and love yourselves as parents in order to accept and love your son or daughter. Do not blame yourselves for a homosexual orientation in your child.

2. Acceptance and love does not mean approving all related attitudes and behavioral choices. You may even challenge a lifestyle you find objectionable.

3. Urge your son or daughter to stay close to the Catholic faith community.

4. Recommend that your child choose a spiritual director.

5. Seek some support for yourself. Consider joining a parents group.

6. Reach out to other parents struggling with a son's or daughter's homosexuality. Does your diocese have a ministry for gay and lesbian Catholics? Does family life ministry provide any direction for parents, engaged couples or newlyweds?

7. Remember, you can only change yourself, not your child.

8. Put your faith in God, who is more powerful and compassionate and more forgiving than we are or could ever be.

Since our bishops have placed homosexuality back into marriage and family life, they have also reminded pastors that they too must address this question with faithfulness to the teachings of the church and a new awareness of how complex homosexual orientation can be to everyone concerned. It is equally important to address how conflicted parishioners can be in their responses to the visibility of homosexual Catholics participating fully in parish life and the presence of mothers and fathers who live with a challenge that has implications for the entire parish community. Once again, I offer a brief sketch of the recommendations to pastors by the bishops. I do so with the hope of making parents aware of what they have a right to expect from the church and from the parish community.

1. Be available.

2. Welcome homosexual persons into the faith community. Never presume that homosexual persons are sexually active.

3. Learn more about homosexuality and church teaching and include some of this in your own preaching.

4. Use the words *homosexual, gay* and *lesbian* in accurate and sensitive ways.

5. Have a list of professional counselors available who are familiar with Catholic teaching and pastoral wisdom.

6. Help establish and encourage support groups.

7. HIV/AIDS is not a gay disease, nor is it God's just punishment. In the United States, although not in the rest of

the world, HIV has disproportionately touched the gay community.

Be sensitive to a family and a community who still mourn deeply.

I would make only one comment here. Because we have been so distanced from homosexual persons, we may feel inept in how to approach them. We may fear adding to the hurt and alienation a homosexual person feels toward the church. We may feel that the whole question is a lost cause because the church is giving too little too late. Or we may feel that nothing we might do is quite enough. We could also fear being patronizing. From my experience, let me offer an encouraging and simple word. Once when Jesus was faced with a vast crowd of hungry people, he suggested that his disciples feed the throng. One of the disciples responded: "We have only two loaves and five fish. What is that among so many?" And Jesus' response was both challenging and revealing: "Share the little you have." Our homosexual children and their parents, who number in the thousands upon thousands of mostly invisible Roman Catholics, hunger and thirst for very little. My experience has been that they just want to be treated as ordinary Catholics. If each of us only gave a bit of kindness and understanding, if we offered even a modicum of inclusiveness, they would be content. And for giving the little we have, the church would be the richer. The little that we have could be as simple as a prayer during the intercessions, an inclusive remark during a homily or a recognition of a deep and lifelong companionship. The little that we have might be a bulletin announcement noting some activity of a diocesan outreach to homosexual Catholics. Maybe the little that we have is keeping a supply of *Always Our Children* in a pamphlet rack in the church vestibule.

I am confident that many homosexual Catholics will read this little book with a good deal of curiosity. I fear that many of their expectations of this book will never be met. What word of hope and encouragement can I offer them?

We are a teaching church. A teaching church is also a learning church. To give the impression, as some do today, that the final word on homosexuality has been spoken by our church is not true, can be misleading and may even reveal a hidden agenda of hostility toward homosexual persons. There is nothing disloyal or unorthodox about candidly admitting that present church teaching on the subject of homosexuality needs our study and pondering. I am not suggesting that there is no truth in present teaching. Nor am I suggesting a radical change of present teaching. What I am saying is that homosexuality is a highly complex reality that admits of serious dilemmas and questions that do not have easy answers or solutions. Deeper insights are always possible as the church listens and ponders on the lived experience of homosexual persons under the constant and sure guidance of the Holy Spirit. The very title of this book is an invitation to deeper discernment. The lives and faith of so many homosexual Catholics who remain in the church are contributing to that discernment. I believe that the bishops were creating and affirming that contribution when they addressed homosexual Catholics at the end of their pastoral letter.

> Though at times you may feel discouraged, hurt or angry, do not walk away from your families, from the Christian community, from all those who love you. In you God's love is revealed. You are always our children.[6]

The clearest presentation I have ever read on homosexuality is by Father Gerald D. Coleman, S.S. The book is called *Homosexuality: Catholic Teaching and Pastoral Practice.*[7]

This same book, while clear and unquestionably true to Catholic teaching, also presents some of the questions and dilemmas that still need to be answered. In the foreword to this book, Cardinal Roger Mahony, Archbishop of Los Angeles, wisely states:

> In dealing with the complex issues surrounding homosexuality, it is very easy to give simple and at times caustic answers. It is much more difficult, but rewarding to travel the journey of wisdom in order to foster a panorama of truth, objectivity and honest sensitivity to human needs and aspirations.[8]

Pope Paul VI once said that genuine dialogue offers a spirit of "meekness": it is not haughty or bitter and does not offend; it is peaceful and avoids violence in word and deed; it is patient and generous. He concludes: "The dialogue will make us wise." Dear reader, let these pages set the stage for the dialogue.

"Here are my mother and my brothers. For whoever does the will of God is my brother and sister and mother."   Mark 3:34–35

Notes

Chapter 1: Everyone Is Talking about It

1. Congregation for the Doctrine of the Faith, *Letter to the Bishops of the Catholic Church on the Pastoral Care of Homosexual Persons, Origins* 16, no. 22 (November 13, 1986): no. 2.
2. NCCB Committee on Marriage and Family Life, *Always Our Children: A Pastoral Message to Parents of Homosexual Children and Suggestions for Pastoral Ministers.* (This is a modification and reissue of the original version, released October 1, 1997.) *Origins* 28, no. 7 (July 2, 1998): p. 102.
3. *Letter to Bishops,* no. 9.
4. *Letter to Bishops,* no. 16.

Chapter 2: Toward a Definition of Homosexuality

1. See also National Conference of Catholic Bishops, *Sharing the Light of Faith: National Catechetical Directory for Catholics in the United States* (Washington, D.C.: United States Catholic Conference, 1979), no. 191; Congregation for Catholic Education, *Educational Guidance in Human Love* (Washington, D.C.: United States Catholic Conference, 1983), no. 4; and National Council of Catholic Bishops, *Human Sexuality: A Catholic Perspective for Education and Lifelong Learning* (Washington, D.C.: United States Catholic Conference, 1991), p. 54.
2. Sigmund Freud, "Letter to an American Mother" (1935), reprinted in Ronald Bayer, *Homosexuality and American Psychiatry* (Princeton: Princeton University Press, 1987), p. 27.
3. George A. Kanoti and Anthony R. Kosnik, *Encyclopedia of Bioethics,* vol. 2 (New York: Free Press 1978), p. 671. See also Wayne R. Dynes, ed., *Encyclopedia of Homosexuality* (New York/London: Garland Publishing, 1992).

4. Congregation for the Doctrine of the Faith, *Letter to the Bishops of the Catholic Church on the Pastoral Care of Homosexual Persons, Origins* 16, no. 22 (November 13, 1986): no. 3.

5. Congregation for the Doctrine of the Faith, *Personae Humanae, Vatican Council II: More Postconciliar Documents,* Vatican Collection, vol. 2, ed. Austin Flannery, O.P. (Northport, N.Y.: Costello Publishing Company).

6. *Letter to Bishops,* no. 16.

7. Ibid.

8 National Conference of Catholic Bishops, *Principles to Guide Confessors in Questions of Homosexuality* (Washington, D.C.: United States Catholic Conference, 1973).

9. Gerald D. Coleman, S.S., "Homosexuals and Spirituality," *Chicago Studies* 32. (November 1993): pp. 222–33.

10. *Human Sexuality,* 1991, p. 54.

11. *Diagnostic and Statistical Manual,* 3rd ed. (Washington, D.C.: American Psychiatric Association, 1980), p. 281.

12. National Conference of Catholic Bishops Committee on Marriage and Family Life, *Always Our Children: A Pastoral Message to Parents of Homosexual Children and Suggestions for Pastoral Ministers* (This is a modification and reissue of the original version, released October 1, 1997.) *Origins* 28, no. 7 (July 2, 1998): pp. 101–2.

Chapter 3: What Does the Bible Teach?

1. Congregation for the Doctrine of the Faith, *Letter to the Bishops of the Catholic Church on the Pastoral Care of Homosexual Persons and Suggestions for Pastoral Ministers* (This is a modification and reissue of the original version, released October 1, 1997.), *Origins* 16, no. 22 (November 13, 1986): nos. 6–7.

2. All scripture texts are taken from the New American Bible with Revised New Testament, 1986, 1970, Confraternity of Christian Doctrine, Inc. Washington, D.C.

3. *Letter to Bishops,* no. 5.

Chapter 4: Homosexuality and Catholic Teaching

1. Congregation for the Doctrine of the Faith, *Declaration on Certain Questions Concerning Sexual Ethics* (Washington, D.C.: United States Catholic Conference, 1975), no. 59.

2. Pope John Paul II, *The Splendor of Truth (Veritatis Splendor), Origins* 23 (1993): no. 80.

3. National Conference of Catholic Bishops Committee on Pastoral Research and Practices, *Principles to Guide Confessors in Questions of Homosexuality* (Washington, D.C.: United States Catholic Conference, 1973), no. 5.

4. National Council of Catholic Bishops, *Human Sexuality: A Catholic Perspective for Education and Lifelong Learning* (Washington, D.C.: United States Catholic Conference, 1991), p. 54.

5. National Conference of Catholic Bishops, *Sharing the Light of Faith: National Catechetical Directory for Catholics in the United States* (Washington, D.C.: United States Catholic Conference, 1977, no. 191.

6. *Principles to Guide Confessors in Questions of Homosexuality,* nos. 8–9.

7. Ibid., nos. 10–11.

8. Ibid., no. 11.

9. National Conference of Catholic Bishops, *To Live in Christ Jesus: A Pastoral Reflection on the Moral Life* (Washington: D.C.: United States Catholic Conference 1976), no. 52.

10. *Declaration on Certain Questions Concerning Sexual Ethics,* no. 8.

11. Congregation for the Doctrine of the Faith, *Letter to the Bishops of the Catholic Church on the Pastoral Care of Homosexual Persons. Origins* 16, no. 22 (November 13, 1986): no. 3.

12. Ibid.

13. John R. Quinn, "Toward an Understanding of the Letter on the Pastoral Care of Homosexual Persons," *America* 156 (1987): p. 94

14. *Letter to the Bishops of the Catholic Church on the Pastoral Care of Homosexual Persons,* no. 11.

15. *Catechism of the Catholic Church.* ([Libreria Editrice Vaticana]:

Washington, D.C.: United States Catholic Conference, 1994/ 1997), nos. 2357–59.

Chapter 5: The Origins of Homosexuality

1. Judith A. Reisman and Edward W. Eichel, *Kinsey, Sex, and Fraud: The Indoctrination of a People* (Lafayette, La.: Huntington House, 1990) pp. 62–63.

2. *Pastoral Constitution on the Church in the Modern World (Gaudium et Spes)* 1965. *Vatican Council II: More Postconciliar Documents,* Vatican Collection, vol. 1 (Northport, N.Y.: Costello Publishing Co., 1992), ed. Austin Flannery, O.P., no 64.

3. Gerald D. Coleman, S.S., *Homosexuality, Catholic Teaching and Pastoral Practice* (Mahwah, N.J. Paulist Press, 1995), p. 207.

4. For more information on this topic, see Marcia Baringa, "Is Homosexuality Biological?" *Science* 253 (1991): 956–57 and "Differences in Brain Structure May Cause Homosexuality," in *Homosexuality: Opposing Viewpoints,* ed. William Dudley (San Diego, Calif.: Greenhaven Press, 1993), pp. 17–22.

5. See Sandra Witelson, "Homosexuality and Cognition," *Briefings* 539 (1992): p. 30.

6. Richard C. Pillard, "Does Homosexuality Have a Biological Basis?" *Research News* 33 (1992): pp. 5–6.

7. Ibid.

8. Eric Marcus, *Is It a Choice?* (San Francisco: Harper, 1993), pp. 10–11. For the study itself, see Dean H. Hamer, Stella Hu, Victoria L. Magnuson, Nan Hu and Angela M.L. Pattatucci, "A Linkage between DNA Markers on the X Chromosome and Male Sexual Orientation," *Science* 261 (1993): pp. 321–27.

Chapter 6: I Choose to Stay in the Church

1. Andrew Sullivan, *Virtually Normal* (New York: Vintage Books, 1995), pp. 6–7.

Chapter 8: "Always Our Children"

1. National Council of Catholic Bishops, *Human Sexuality: A Catholic Perspective for Education and Lifelong Learning* (Washington, D.C.: United States Catholic Conference, 1991), p. 56.
2. Ibid.
3. Eric Marcus, *Is It a Choice?* (San Francisco: Harper, 1993), pp. 29, 33.
4. NCCB Committee on Marriage and Family Life. *Always Our Children: A Pastoral Message to Parents of Homosexual Children and Suggestions for Pastoral Ministers* (This is a modification and reissue of the original version, released October 1, 1997.) *Origins* 28, no. 7 (July 2, 1998).
5. Ibid., p. 99.
6. Ibid., p. 102.
7. Gerald D. Coleman, S.S., *Homosexuality: Catholic Teaching and Pastoral Practice* (Mahwah, N.J.: Paulist Press, 1995), p. 207.
8. Ibid., p. viii.

Bibliography

Barinaga, Marcia. "Differences in Brain Structure May Cause Homosexuality." In *Homosexuality: Opposing Viewpoints.* William Dudley, ed. San Diego, Calif.: Greenhaven Press, 1993.

————. "Is Homosexuality Biological?" *Science* 253 (1991).

Bayer, Ronald. *Homosexuality and American Psychiatry.* Princeton: Princeton University Press, 1987.

Catechism of the Catholic Church. Libreria Editrice Vaticana. Washington, D.C.: United States Catholic Conference, 1994/1997.

Coleman, Gerald D. *Homosexuality: Catholic Teaching and Pastoral Practice.* Mahwah, N.J.: Paulist Press, 1995.

————. "Homosexuals and Spirituality." *Chicago Studies* 32 (November 1993): 222–33.

Congregation for Catholic Education. *Educational Guidance in Human Love.* Washington, D.C.: United States Catholic Conference, 1983.

Congregation for the Doctrine of the Faith. *Declaration on Certain Questions Concerning Sexual Ethics (Personae Humanae). Vatican Council II: More Postconciliar Documents.* Vatican Collection, vol. 2. Austin Flannery, O.P., ed. Northport, N.Y.: Costello Publishing Company, 1982.

————. *Letter to the Bishops of the Catholic Church on the Pastoral Care of Homosexual Persons.* Washington, D.C.: United States Catholic Conference, 1986.

Diagnostic and Statistical Manual of Mental Disorders. 3rd ed. Washington, D.C.: American Psychiatric Association, 1980.

Encyclopedia of Homosexuality. Wayne R. Dynes, ed. New York/London: Garland Publishing, 1992.

Freud, Sigmund. "Letter to an American Mother" (1935). In *Homosexuality and American Psychiatry* by Ronald Bayer. Princeton: Princeton University Press, 1987.

Hamer, Dean H., Stella Hu, Victoria L. Magnuson, Nan Hu, Angela M. L. Pattatucci. "A Linkage between DNA Markers on the X Chromosome and Male Sexual Orientation." *Science* 261 (1993): 321–27.

Wittelson, Sandra. "Homosexuality and Cognition." *Briefings* 539 (1992).

Kanoti, George A., and Anthony R. Kosnik. *Encyclopedia of Bioethics.* Vol. 2. New York: Free Press, 1978.

Marcus, Eric. *Is It a Choice?* San Francisco: Harper, 1993.

National Conference of Catholic Bishops. *Called to Compassion and Responsibility: A Response to the HIV/AIDS Crisis.* Washington, D.C.: United States Catholic Conference, 1990.

———. *Human Sexuality: A Catholic Perspective for Education and Lifelong Learning.* Washington, D.C.: United States Catholic Conference, 1991.

———. *Principles to Guide Confessors in Questions of Homosexuality.* Washington, D.C.: United States Catholic Conference, 1978.

———. *Sharing the Light of Faith: National Catechetical Directory for Catholics in the United States.* Washington, D.C.: United States Catholic Conference, 1979.

————. *To Live in Christ Jesus: A Pastoral Reflection on the Moral Life.* Washington, D.C.: United States Catholic Conference, 1996.

National Conference of Catholic Bishops Committee on Marriage and Family Life. *Always Our Children: A Pastoral Message to Parents of Homosexual Children and Suggestions for Pastoral Ministers.* (This is a modification and reissue of the original version, released October 1, 1997.) *Origins* 28, no. 7 (July 2, 1998).

Pillard, Richard C. "Does Homosexuality Have a Biological Basis?" In *Research News* 33 (1992).

Pope John Paul II. *Apostolic Exhortation on the Family (Familiaris Consortio). Vatican Council II: More Postconciliar Documents.* Vatican Collection, vol. 2, Austin Flannery, O.P., ed. Northport, N.Y.: Costello Publishing Company, 1982.

————. *The Splendor of Truth (Veritatis Splendor). Origins* 23 (1993).

Quinn, John R. "Toward the Understanding of the Letter on the Pastoral Care of Homosexual Persons." *America* 156 (1987).

Reisman, Judith A., and Edward W. Eichel. *Kinsey, Sex, and Fraud: The Indoctrination of a People.* Lafayette, La.: Huntington House, 1990.

Sullivan, Andrew. *Virtually Normal.* New York: Vintage Books, 1995.